Methods
of the
Masters

Methods of the Masters
Copyright © 2013 Each author in this book retains the copyright and all inherent rights to their individual chapter. Their stories are printed herein with their permission. Each author is responsible for the individual opinions expressed through their words.
ISBN: 9780984795291

All rights reserved. No part of this publication may be reproduced, distributed, or transmitted in any form or by any means, including photocopying, recording, or other electronic mechanical methods, without the prior written permission of the publisher, except in the case of brief quotations embodied in critical reviews and certain other noncommercial uses permitted by copyright law. For permission requests, write to the publisher, addressed "Attention Permission Coordinator," at the address below.

The authors of this book do not dispense medical advice or prescribe the use of any technique as a form of treatment for physical or medical problems without the advice of a physician, either directly, or indirectly. If the reader chooses to use any of the information in this book, the author and publisher assume no responsibility for their actions.

BECKWORTH PUBLICATIONS

3108 E 10th St ~ Trenton, Mo 64683 ~ 660-204-4088

Ordering information: Quantity Sales. Special discounts are available on quantity purchases by corporations, associations, and others. For details, contact the "Special Sales Department at Beckworth Publications."

Beckworth Publications and the Beckworth Publications logo are trademarks of Beckworth Publications.

Printed in the United States of America.
Library of Congress Cataloging-in-Publication Data.

Methods of the Masters
Library of Congress Control Number: 2013934950

Compiled by: Vince Harris
Cover and Interior Graphic Design: Mike Baugher

Table of Contents

Foreword

Chapter 1 ~ Help for Depression   4
Jillian Coleman Wheeler

Chapter 2 ~ Depths of Discovery   18
Elaine Lemon

Chapter 3 ~ Courage Can Come from Darkness:
Overcoming Fear to Create a Life You Love   52
Blanca Cobb

Chapter 4 ~ It's All About Relationships   64
Cheri Najor

Chapter 5 ~ Biggest Nightmare or Biggest Gift?   74
Kathryn Orford

Chapter 6 ~ No Room for Fear   86
Kim Rinaldi Robey

Chapter 7 ~ Catalyst for Change   97
Kimberly Pratte

Chapter 8 ~ It's Time to Get Real   106
Lisa Schilling

Chapter 9 ~ Re-create Your Life   123
Robyn Podboy

Chapter 10 ~ The Doctor of the Future is You   133
Sabrina Peterson

FOREWORD

Kirsty TV is all about the power of sharing stories. I believe when people share their stories they heal themselves and they heal others. So I was thrilled to be invited to write the Foreword for this book.

Whether you've just dipped your toes in the water of Personal Development or are a seasoned student, I know you'll enjoy reading and benefit greatly from *Methods of the Masters*.

"Life" doesn't come with an instruction manual. And let's face it, sometimes the going gets tough!

I don't know what challenges you're dealing with in your life right now, but what I do know is that you'll find a smorgasbord of tools, techniques and exercises in this book to assist you to deal with all of those challenges and in the process transform your life.

So find a comfy sofa and get started today!

Kirsty

Kirsty Spraggon
Kirsty TV
www.kirstytv.com
International Speaker
Author of "Work as if you Own it"
NSAA BreakThrough Speaker of the Year
RE/MAX Hall of Fame ~ Top 1% Individuals Worldwide

ENDORSEMENTS FOR JILLIAN COLEMAN WHEELER

"Help for Depression" is a wonderful contribution to *Methods of the Masters*. Well written, informative, and personal, it's a riveting read. Most of all, it contains hope and information that everyone needs. I am happy to recommend it.

- Joe Vitale, Ph.D. Author of the international #1 best-seller, *The Attractor Factor*, the #1 best-seller *Life's Missing Instruction Manual*, the #1 best-selling e-book *Hypnotic Writing*, and the #1 best-selling *Nightingale-Conant* audio program, *The Power of Outrageous Marketing*, among numerous other works. Dr. Vitale is also one of the stars of the hit movie *The Secret*.

"The best self help books are written by those who have successfully journeyed ahead of you toward wellness. *Methods of the Masters* is such a resource, particularly the chapter, "Help for Depression." Jillian Coleman Wheeler is an empathic, seasoned veteran of the wars we all fight. She's been on both sides of the recovery equation. This book will equip you with the armament needed to conquer doubts and trouble and to achieve success."

- L.B. Hodge, M.A., M.F.A., Ph.D.
  Professor of Behavioral Science (retired), Acclaimed Poet, Author and Consultant
  Author: *Heartsongs: Recovery from Grief, Loss and Trauma*
  VeteranTraveler.com

"The moment I began reading "Help for Depression," by Jillian Coleman Wheeler, I could not put the article down. Her self-disclosing style pulls the reader in, and makes one want to keep right on reading. It was her openness and pure, brutal honesty that kept me fascinated, even more than the facts and scientific research. And, I am a research scientist! She does not claim to have a system with just one approach and a "one cure fits all." Jillian mentions the drugs she has taken, meditation, nutrients and the importance of lifestyle changes. Her expertise is personal as well as professional. At one point, Jillian writes, "I decided, on a deep, bedrock basis, to take suicide off the table as an option." If you or someone you love is facing depression, you need to get your hands on *Methods of the Masters* and read "Help for Depression."

- Dr. Gayle Joplin Hall, Author, Lifestyle Coach, and Mentor
  DrHallonCall.com - Private Coaching and Services
  DrHallonCallCoaching.com - Group Coaching Services

"The sun stopped shining for me is all. The whole story is: I am sad. I am sad all the time and the sadness is so heavy that I can't get away from it. Not ever." - Nina LaCour, Hold Still

Chapter 1

Help for Depression

There was a time in my life I thought I was the only severely depressed person on the planet. That's not too surprising, since depression is a disease characterized by feelings of self-absorption and isolation.

In addition, depressed people wear masks. We tend to walk through the world quietly, nodding and smiling and functioning, more or less. We're often ashamed of our depression, and it seems pointless and overwhelming to try to explain to anyone else how we really feel.

But I wasn't the only one. And if you are depressed, neither are you. According to a 2011 study published by Medco Health Solutions, one in four American women is taking psychotropic medications- primarily antidepressants. If that many women are on drugs, how many women are pursuing alternative treatments, or simply have not been diagnosed? And what about men? The National Institutes of Health tells us that one in eight men suffers from depression.

That's an epidemic.

This is the story of my depression and my eventual recovery. Depression differs in type and severity, so my depression story may be very different from yours, or that of your friend or family member. There is also a great deal of practical information here about the disease and the many approaches to healing. Today, more than ever in the past, there is genuine help for depression.

I was first diagnosed as severely depressed when I was hospitalized after considering suicide. I didn't make a bona fide attempt at suicide, but I found myself driving down the road at night thinking about pulling into oncoming traffic. Fortunately, some small sane voice inside screamed back at me, and I stopped on the side of the road before I killed myself or anyone else.

Over the years, that little voice saved my life a number of times. It pulled me back from the edge when I had a handful of sleeping pills, and when I had the barrel of a gun in my mouth.

Writing about it now, separated from that period of my life by years of relative sanity, it's hard to imagine I was that crazy. Because of course, it is crazy to consider killing yourself, right?

To someone who has never suffered from an acute form of depression, the idea of suicide may indeed seem inherently insane. But is it insane to consider suicide if you are faced with an incurable, excruciatingly painful disease? The pain of depression, while certainly different than physical pain, is just as terrible for the sufferer to contemplate. In 2008, 37,000 Americans succeeded in committing suicide. 666,000 Americans were treated in hospitals for self-inflicted injuries.

That's a lot of pain.

I was twenty-six years old when I was admitted to the psychiatric hospital. I'd been in counseling before- marriage counseling, then individual and group therapy. I was diagnosed then with "Adult Adjustment Disorder." That's a great catchall diagnosis, because, after all, adulthood is in part a process of learning to adjust to what is.

But the psych ward was the real deal. It was my first opportunity to tell the truth to anyone about how much I was really hurting. It was the safest I had ever felt up to that point in my life, and the most I had ever been able to relax.

Everyone in my life outside the hospital was confused. How had I fallen apart like this? And how fast could I get back to normal?

My husband was stunned. He knew I was emotional and cried a lot, but how could I breach our contract and disappear into a loony bin? My children, who had rarely been separated from me, felt upset and abandoned. When they all visited, these people I loved so much, I felt as though I was seeing them through layers of gauze.

When I called my boss, I could tell he was worried about me. Nevertheless, instead of supporting me in getting help, he put huge pressure on me to get out as soon as possible and get back to work on my projects. When I returned to my job, the whole subject was quickly swept under the rug. My boss believed mental illness was shameful, and with my best interests at heart, he tried to hide the situation.

Upon my release, I began seeing the psychiatrist who had treated me in the hospital. I met with him several times a week. He knew how sick I was, so I didn't have to stay in my role as the competent, confident young woman who had everything under control. For the first time, I began to talk honestly about my life and my mental health. I began, in a small way, to live in a new kind of integrity.

What is Depression?

The term "depression" is actually an umbrella for a variety of emotional conditions. There are a number of types of depression that have been identified, and it's helpful to have a basic understanding of them.

Situational Depression is a normal human response to life circumstances. When we suffer a loss, we experience grief, and depression is a predictable aspect of grief. So if someone we love dies or leaves us, or if we lose a job or a home, a period of depression is only natural. If the depression continues for more than a month or two, however, it becomes a mental health issue.

Chronic Depression, also known as Dysthymia, is a long-standing condition which lasts more than a year. The person with Chronic Depression is generally able to carry on with the tasks of daily life, despite a constant feeling of sadness. The person, or other people close to him, may notice a marked lack of enthusiasm in all situations, weight gain or loss, and constant fatigue. This type of depression is dangerous because, while the sufferer may be going about her usual activities, she may actually have lost hope, and be at risk of slipping into a Major Depression.

Major Depression is an acute form of the disease, characterized by feelings of deep sadness and abject hopelessness, often accompanied by extreme guilt and a sense of inadequacy. Physical symptoms may include exhaustion and pain. The person may cry constantly, or may withdraw into himself. Thoughts of suicide are common. Loss of interest in sex and changes in sleeping and eating patterns are also typical in episodes of Major Depression. Some people may experience only a single episode in a lifetime, but it is more common to have recurrent episodes. This type of illness can be diagnosed if it lasts longer than two weeks. If you or someone you know experiences a Major Depression, it is important to seek help immediately. Despite the severity of the symptoms, Major Depression now responds to treatment in eighty to ninety percent of cases.

Postpartum Depression happens after a woman has given birth. It has been estimated that eighty-five percent of new mothers have "the baby blues," a time during which they feel overwhelmed and sad. After all, delivering and assuming total responsibility for a helpless infant is an enormous undertaking. However, an estimated thirteen percent of women experience a depression serious enough to require immediate intervention, probably in response to extreme hormone shifts. These women feel isolated and inadequate, exhausted and often unable to bond with their babies. They may be suicidal, and often have fears of hurting their infants.

If you suspect that you, or a woman you know, is more depressed than seems normal after childbirth, seek help immediately. Most physicians are now better informed than in the past about Postpartum Depression, but if you feel your doctor is not taking you seriously, find one who will. Enlist your husband, your mother, or a friend to accompany you and advocate for you.

Seasonal Affective Disorder, or SAD, seems to be stimulated by a lack of full-spectrum light. People with SAD typically experience a loss of energy and enthusiasm, and feelings of sadness, fatigue and often weight gain, during the winter months. SAD can usually be successfully treated with light therapy.

About forty percent of depressed people can be diagnosed with Atypical Depression (which raises the question, why isn't it called "typical"?). These people may become depressed as a result of feeling rejected, and they tend to sleep and eat to excess. Unlike people with Dysthymia and Major Depression, people with Atypical Depression often rally and feel better in response to positive events in their lives.

In an estimated ten to fifteen percent of cases, depression can be so extreme that it includes delusions and hallucinations, which cause the person to imagine or even see and hear things that don't exist in reality. This is called Psychotic Depression, and because the symptoms are so far outside ordinary behavior, people close to the sufferer usually notice and encourage him or her to get medical attention.

Premenstrual Dysphoric Disorder, or PMDD, can be described as "PMS on steroids." Like premenstrual syndrome, it affects women during the second half of their menstrual cycle, but the symptoms of depression are much more pronounced. While approximately seventy-five percent of menstruating women experience some degree of PMS, about five percent suffer from PMDD.

Imagine that human emotions exist across a range between two poles, from very high to very low, with a point in the middle that represents our average experience. Each of the types of depression mentioned above is a "unipolar" depression. That is, the mood of the depressed person descends from average to very low. But there is another type of depression, Bipolar Disorder, which manifests as Bipolar I or Bipolar II.

Bipolar Disorder used to be called Manic Depressive Illness, because the sufferer's moods range from manic (very high and excited) to depressed (very low). During periods of mania, the person may believe he is invincible, full of brilliant ideas and impervious to failure. The manic person may gamble compulsively, spend all his money on impulse purchases, or act out sexually. Then, he crashes into a deep depression. In Bipolar II, the manic episodes are much less intense. The "cycling" from one mood to another may take place as infrequently as a few times a year, or in some cases there may be "rapid cycling" where moods change within moments. The brain chemistry of Bipolar Disorder is different than unipolar depressions, and requires different interventions.

I used to joke that I wished I had a bipolar, rather than a unipolar depression; at least I'd have had some up times. In reality, however, Bipolar Disorder is no joking matter. Bipolar sufferers endure deep episodes of depression, and in addition they must deal with the likely consequences of their manic behavior.

My type of depression is Dysthymia, and during various periods of my life I have had recurrent episodes of Major Depression. This combination is sometimes called "Double Depression."

How Do You Know for Sure?

Later on, as a counselor, I learned that many people are not sure if they are truly depressed. After all, changes in moods are normal. There will always be times when even the healthiest people feel a little blue. How do you know if you (or someone close to you) are depressed, and need help?

Because depression is a complex condition with a variety of possible symptoms, it is advisable to get a professional diagnosis. But it is possible, and often helpful, to begin with a self-assessment.

The following is a test developed by Dr. Ivan K. Goldberg, a New York psychiatrist and clinical psychopharmacologist who specializes in working with depressed patients. In addition to providing baseline information, the test can also be a useful way to periodically assess whether the symptoms of depression are improving or getting worse. Any change of 5 points or more in either direction is considered to be significant.

The Goldberg Depression Test:

Points are assigned to each question as follows:
Not at all (0) A little (1) Somewhat (2) Moderately (3) Quite a lot (4) Very much (5)

Once all the questions are answered, the scores are added up to give a final score and an indication of the likelihood of depression.

Depression Test Questions:

1. I do things slowly.
2. My future appears hopeless.
3. It is hard for me to concentrate on reading.
4. The pleasure and fun has gone out of my life.
5. I find it hard to make decisions.
6. I have lost interest in things that used to be important to me.
7. I feel unhappy, depressed and sad.
8. I feel agitated and unable to relax.
9. I feel tired.
10. It takes a lot of effort for me to do simple things.
11. I feel guilty and I deserve to be punished.
12. I feel like a failure.
13. I feel numb and lifeless, more dead than alive.
14. My sleep is disturbed; I'm sleeping too much or too little.
15. I spend time thinking how I can commit suicide.
16. I feel trapped or confined.
17. I feel depressed even when good things happen to me.
18. I have lost weight or put it on without being on a diet.

Scoring on the Goldberg Depression Test:

A score of 9 or above indicates the presence of depression.
Between 10 and 17 - possibly some minor depression
Between 18 and 21 – maybe on the verge of depression
Between 22 and 35 –indication of minor to moderate depression
Between 36 and 53 - moderate to severe depression possible
Over 54 - possibly suffering from severe depression.

Depression may affect men and women quite differently. While women are apt to cry, men may simply seem angry or irritable. We are all socialized in different ways, by our families and by our cultures.

Dr. Goldberg also developed the following screening instrument for Bipolar Disorder:

Goldberg Test for Bipolar Disorder:

This test applies only to persons over eighteen years of age who report feelings of depression.

Points are assigned to each question as follows:
Not at all (0) A little (1) Somewhat (2) Moderately (3) Quite a lot (4) Very much (5)

Once all the questions are answered, the scores are added up to give a final score and an indication of the likelihood of Bipolar Disorder.

Bipolar Disorder Test Questions:

1. At times I am much more talkative or speak much faster than usual.
2. There have been times when I was much more active or did many more things than usual.
3. I get into moods where I feel very speeded up or irritable.
4. There have been times when I have felt both high (elated) and low (depressed) at the same time.
5. At times I have been much more interested in sex than usual.
6. My self-confidence ranges from great self-doubt to equally great overconfidence.
7. There have been great variations in the quantity or quality of my work.
8. For no obvious reason I sometimes have been very angry or hostile.
9. Sometimes I am mentally dull and at other times I think very creatively.
10. At times I am greatly interested in being with people and at other times I just want to be left alone with my thoughts.
11. At some times I have great optimism and at other times equally great pessimism.
12. Some of the time I show much tearfulness and crying and at other times I laugh and joke excessively.

Scoring on the Goldberg Bipolar Disorder Test:

Score of 15 or less – probable unipolar Major Depression
Score between 16 and 24 – indicative of Major Depression or a disorder in the Bipolar Spectrum
Score of 25 or over - very high likelihood Bipolar Disorder is present.

      These tests, while providing helpful information, are not definitive. If you believe you or someone close to you is suffering from any form of depression, consult a health provider. There are many possible courses of treatment from which you can choose, and I will be discussing those here, but the place to begin is with a solid diagnosis.

What We Know Now, that We Didn't Know Then

      I was first diagnosed with Major Depression nearly forty years ago. A few years after that, when I was well enough, I went back to school to become a counselor and to work with clients. My training was in family therapy as well as a variety of other modalities. The director of the institute I attended, however, was a Freudian analyst. In those days, when Dr. Freud's teachings were considered the gold standard, most psychiatrists believed all mental illness was strictly psychological in origin.

For example, we were taught that schizophrenia was caused by overanxious, controlling mothers. Since only about 1.1% of the population is schizophrenic and everybody knows more than one percent of mothers are anxious and controlling, many practitioners questioned this theory.

This is a little therapist humor, but you can see why we had our doubts. Many of us were beginning to question whether mental illness was not at least as much about dysfunction of the brain itself, as about dysfunctional parenting. We were also seeing the positive results of many new and innovative therapeutic approaches.

A little history may be helpful here. While human beings have always exhibited and observed mental illness, until the nineteenth century, the standard of care was to separate the patient from society. Mentally ill people were either kept at home out of sight, or locked in asylums.

From the time Sigmund Freud developed his groundbreaking theories around the turn of the twentieth century, through the 1930s, depression was not recognized as a unique disease, or differentiated from other forms of mental illness.

Patients who were abnormally sad often spent years in treatment, dissecting their childhoods and delving into their unconscious minds. When talk therapy failed to achieve results or when the symptoms of depression became too severe, patients were sometimes placed in mental hospitals, where they might be treated with electroshock therapy. ECT, or electroconvulsive therapy, delivers electricity directly to the brain and induces seizures. In the early days of the treatment beginning in the 1930s, the treatment was a terrifying ordeal. Patients were often treated without anesthesia, and while severe depression was sometimes alleviated, there was a significant risk of memory loss and other side effects.

In 1949, the National Institute of Mental Health was founded in the United States. Its purpose was to foster solid research into mental illness and to develop possible cures. In the 1950s, chemistry had advanced to the point that drug companies had been formed and drugs were being developed for all kinds of disease. In the beginning, the discovery of drugs that helped depression was accidental.

For example, patients reported that the drug Iproniazid, which was used in the treatment of tuberculosis, caused an improvement in mood. These discoveries encouraged continued research and the eventual development of other drugs. In 1950, researchers searching for a drug to treat psychotic patients developed Imipramine, the first Tricyclic antidepressant. Tricyclics provided a measure of relief to some depressed patients, as did the early MAOIs (monoamine oxidase inhibitors), but with both types of drugs, there were often significant side effects.

Today we are in a new age of treatment for depression, as well as a host of other mental illnesses. With the advent of PET Scans (positron emission tomography) and MRIs (magnetic resonance imaging), scientists are now able to study the actual structure of the brain and how that structure is affected by our thoughts and emotions, and even the events we experience. Scientific research has increased our understanding of genetics and of the electrochemical functioning of the brain, particularly how the levels of various chemicals within the brain affect mental health.

In the 1980s, a revolutionary new class of medicines for depression was developed. These medications are called SSRIs, or Selective Serotonin Reuptake Inhibitors. Serotonin is one of the primary brain chemicals necessary for optimal functioning of mood regulation, and the SSRIs increase its availability in the brain. SNRIs (Serotonin-Norepinephrine Reuptake Inhibitors) also act upon the brain chemical, norepinephrine.

We now know that depression often presents with anxiety, panic disorder, or in some cases OCD (Obsessive Compulsive Disorder). PTSD(Post-Traumatic Stress Disorder) may also accompany depression. Understanding the symptoms of these mental health disorders can help therapists in treatment, as well as the clients themselves.

Over the past thirty years, a variety of related drugs have been developed, many attempting to target and affect other brain chemicals and specific aspects of brain function. In addition, there are newer MAOIs that have fewer side effects than the originals, and that are sometimes useful in treating Atypical Depression.

We also know now that the brain is "plastic," that it is constantly changing and adapting to our life circumstances and emotions. For example, it has been demonstrated that in the brains of medical students, who must memorize enormous amounts of material, the area of the brain that governs memory increases in size. It has been proven that under great stress, parts of the brain shut down to allow the mind to focus solely on survival.

It is likely that children who live in pain and under stress are more apt to become depressed, but we also know that when depression is alleviated, the brain grows new neurons and makes new connections. The brain heals itself.

We also know that not all depression is the result of a tragic history. Some depression is undoubtedly genetic. There was probably an element of that in my own history, as my mother was hospitalized in her thirties with what was then called a "nervous breakdown."

My Path to Healing

I would like to be able to say that my hospitalization and the ensuing therapy cured my depression, but in truth, over another decade went by before I really got better. The crisis that put me in the hospital was an important turning point, however, because it forced me to understand that I wasn't just a sad person. I was really sick, and if I was going to have the life I wanted, I would have to commit myself to getting well.

Upon my release, my psychiatrist wrote me a prescription for a tricyclic antidepressant. In those days, it was the best medication available, but, except for making me sick to my stomach, confused and sleepy, it was useless. Unlike the Freudian psychiatrists I mentioned earlier, this doctor was progressive and action-oriented in his therapeutic approach. We met together for therapy for a number of months, and the work we did had great value for me.

My childhood was a troubled one. My mother was an alcoholic, and my father was violent and sadistic. They were both self-absorbed, and because I was the oldest child, I bore the brunt of their problems. My father in particular, was undoubtedly damaged by his experiences in World War II. He abused me severely and my mother, who saw me as competition, encouraged the abuse. At the same time, they were too preoccupied with their own emotional struggles and the challenge of raising a young family, to provide much positive attention.

Eventually I had six younger siblings, and I tried in every way to protect them. In therapy, I came to see that I had taken on the roles of both the hero and the victim. I felt I was in charge of keeping everyone around me safe, and yet I felt helpless to save myself. As is usually the case with children of alcoholics, I carried great guilt. If only I were a better person, or somehow magically more capable, I believed, I could rescue my mother from her unhappiness and win the attention of my father.

My psychiatrist listened patiently for a few weeks, and then he began to confront the assumptions upon which I'd based my whole life. In one session, particularly, he turned my world upside down. Ironically, I always knew my father loved me, despite the abuse. But I never felt love from my mother, and I was constantly seeking her approval and affection.

"Your mother doesn't love you," the doctor announced. "She never loved you, because she's simply not capable of that kind of mothering. So you're wasting your time trying to win her love. It's time to give up, and start taking care of yourself instead."

I was stunned. I began to see the world, and my role in it, completely differently. I began to assume responsibility for my own choices, and my own happiness. I came to realize that I had married my husband because, although he was quite emotionally distant, he showed me as much affection as I was able to accept at the time. When I began to love myself more and to want a more nurturing relationship, he did not have that to offer. He was a good man, and in all fairness, there is little joy in being married to someone who is severely depressed. But I was moving forward, and he was on a different track.

Within a couple of years, I had gotten a divorce, gone back to school, and changed my career entirely. I continued to work on myself, with several different therapists. In my own training, I got to be the guinea pig for a variety of exciting new approaches to therapy.

From the time I was a child, into my early thirties, I had terrifying nightmares, and I often had episodes in which I would seem to re-experience incidents of abuse. These episodes left me curled up in a corner, sobbing and hyperventilating. As I learned about the treatment of Viet Nam War veterans, I realized that I myself was slowly recovering from Post-Traumatic Stress Syndrome.

I should say here that over the years, I came to forgive my mother and father, and to understand they had done the best they could with the tools they had as parents. In her later years, my mother stopped drinking, and we developed a somewhat closer relationship. A few times, as I listened to her recounting her stories of young motherhood, I caught glimpses of the love she may have wanted to show me, if she'd known how. She herself, however, had been raised by a series of nannies and had a distant relationship with her own mother.

In addition to distinct mood changes, I learned to recognize the other symptoms of my depression. When my mood would begin to drop, one of the first signs was confusion, and an inability to think clearly. For example, despite the fact I had been in advanced math classes in school, I would suddenly no longer be able to do simple arithmetic calculations. Making decisions seemed overwhelming, and I often had trouble remembering how to do simple tasks.

Throughout these years, my depression ebbed and flowed. When the circumstances of my life were going well, it was manageable. But when there was stress, I would sink deeper into despair.

One summer, when I was having a difficult time financially and emotionally, I sent my children to stay with my sister. During that summer, I was constantly on the verge of suicide, and I was frightened that I was not going to be around to finish raising my kids.

That was the summer I began to study meditation, which would prove to be one of the best tools I had to regulate my moods. I also learned that exercise helped me to maintain more emotional stability. When I walked every day and did yoga, the endorphins my body produced acted as natural antidepressants. Regular sleeping habits, as well as sufficient sleep, seemed to have a positive effect.

I began to notice that my deepest depressions occurred in cycles, and for several years I charted the course of my symptoms. There was quite a bit of interest at the time in pre-menstrual syndrome, and a murder defendant in Great Britain even offered PMS as a defense in her case. I could see that my own depression correlated to my hormonal fluctuations.

In 1981, I was working in a hospital and I made an appointment with the Chief of Psychiatry. I took my records, discussed with him the conclusions I had drawn, and asked him if he could suggest any chemical or hormonal intervention that might help me. He didn't completely dismiss my ideas, but he told me he would have to take me on as a patient and see me for at least a couple of years before he would be willing to try any non-traditional approach. By this time, of course, I had trained as a therapist and had worked with clients for a number of years. I shook my head and said, "No, thanks."

A couple of days later I was talking about the situation to my internist (who worked at the same hospital), expressing my frustration. He thought for a moment, and said, "You know, a drug salesman came into my office yesterday with some totally new kind of drug for depression. We'd have to monitor you closely for side effects, but if you want to, we could give it a try."

The drug was Desyrel (a brand name for trazodone), one of the earliest medications to target the brain's serotonin system. Within a week of starting the drug, I felt truly sane for the first time in my life. My mood was consistently high from morning to night, day after day after day. I wasn't manic, simply normal, as I had imagined normal to be. I felt relaxed, comfortably energetic, and I was thinking clearly and rationally.

I remained on Desryrel for almost three years, despite the fact I am generally averse to prescription medications. Although some people had reported success using the herb St. Johns Wort to combat depression, it had not been helpful to me. The Desryel worked, wonderfully.

During those three years I developed frequent bladder spasms. Despite a number of tests, the urologist was unable to determine the cause. Later, it would be acknowledged that bladder spasms were among the many possible side effects of antidepressant medications. Other side effects may include nausea, rashes, impotence, difficulty achieving orgasm, drowsiness, weight gain, headaches and diarrhea.

The reason I eventually stopped taking Desryel was that I wanted to have another baby, and the drug was contraindicated during pregnancy. Fortunately, during this period I had begun to see a Ph.D. nutritionist who encouraged me to substitute the drug with an amino acid, the nutritional supplement, L-Tryptophan, which is what the body uses to manufacture serotonin. Under his supervision, I easily transitioned to L-Tyrptophan, and determined the daily dosage necessary to keep my depression in remission.

L-Tryptophan worked well during my pregnancy and three subsequent years of breastfeeding. Then, in 1989, a batch of the supplement was contaminated at the factory where it was produced in Japan, and it was pulled from the marketplace. I went on Wellbutrin for a brief period of time, and then was able to travel to Canada to obtain L-Tryptophan by prescription. Eventually it again became available over the counter in the U.S.

With the exception of that interruption, I have remained on the same regimen for twenty-seven years. I take L-Tryptophan every day. I walk and exercise regularly. I try to sleep eight hours every night. I meditate every day, virtually without fail. I eat a healthy diet with little sugar.

I consider my spiritual life to be a critical component of my recovery. I grew up Catholic, but today I am much more eclectic in my beliefs. So, I pray; I ask God (or the Universe, or my Higher Power, or whatever term is most comfortable for you) for help in staying healthy. I ask for the things I need and want in life, and I write them down in positive terms. I now believe, and my life experience has borne out, that good things can and do happen for me.

One thing that I no longer worry about is the possibility of committing suicide, even when I go through a low period and the thought occasionally crosses my mind. Even before I went on medication for the first time and really started to get well, I made a life decision. I decided, on a deep, bedrock basis, to take suicide off the table as an option. As a therapist, I had seen too many families enduring unimaginable pain as a result of suicide, and I made up my mind that I would never inflict that on the people who loved me.

The greatest challenge I've experienced during these past twenty-seven years is menopause. The hormonal changes that accompanied that transition threw my carefully crafted regimen off balance. In addition to hot flashes and anxiety attacks, I found myself unable to sleep, and I began to experience much more low-level depression. Eventually I added another amino acid supplement, L-Tyrosine, to my arsenal to counter the anxiety, and I began taking bio-identical hormones to regulate my sleep patterns.

What Can You Expect?

If you are ready to get help for depression, or if you are in a position to support someone you know in getting help, your path will be easier than mine. The enormous leap forward in knowledge about depression has provided a wealth of new tools you can use to get better.

Begin by finding a therapist with whom you feel comfortable. Some psychiatrists only prescribe and supervise medication, and coordinate and consult with the therapist doing ongoing talk therapy. Others perform both functions. If you have health insurance, your insurance company will have a list of providers. If you do not, call the United Way in your community and ask about free or sliding-scale therapy resources. Get recommendations from people you trust. Whether or not you know it, some of your friends and acquaintances have undoubtedly consulted a therapist at some point in their lives.

The type of therapy that has proven most useful for depression is called Cognitive Behavioral Therapy. It works on the premise that what we think and what we tell ourselves stimulates our emotions. Learning new ways of thinking and perceiving the world (as I did so many years ago) is critical to staying healthy.

If your depression is acute, don't be afraid to begin with medication. Your immediate task is to save your life, to begin your return to full functioning, and to reclaim your happiness.

There are several suicide hotlines. Here are two of them:
National Suicide Prevention Hotline: 1-800-273-TALK (1-800-273-8255)
National Hopeline Network: 1-800-SUICIDE (1-800-784-2433)
If you or someone you know needs immediate help, call one of them now.

Explore all the natural options. Like me, you may find a nutritional approach that works for you. There are nutritionists, homeopaths, naturopaths, chiropractors, acupuncturists, and many other healthcare providers who have helped in alleviating depression.

Once your depression has lightened and you are once again able to think clearly and make good decisions, become aware of the signs and symptoms of impending mood changes. You are the expert on your own body and mind.

It will take time and effort on your part; all your problems will not be solved immediately. However, your life will get better and better.

There is help for depression, and you deserve that help. Reach out for it now.

Jillian Coleman Wheeler © 2012, Used with Permission by Beckworth Publications, *Methods of the Masters*.

Jillian Coleman Wheeler

Jillian Coleman Wheeler is a writer and speaker with a background in counseling and consulting. She has a successful Internet business training grant writers, and is the co-author (with her friend Joe Vitale) of *Your Internet Cash Machine: The Insiders' Guide to Making Big Money, Fast*, published by Wiley New York. In addition, Jillian is a contributing author to the books *Meet and Grow Rich, Million Dollar Emails, Volume II*; *Life's Missing Instruction Manual*, and *Life Lessons for Mastering the Law of Attraction* (A Chicken Soup for the Soul book). She's currently at work on a full-length book about overcoming depression.

Jillian is also the creator of Your Roadmap to Riches, a powerful process for creating an abundant life. Her essays on personal growth and spirituality, as well as some of her poetry, are available through her website, JillianColemanWheeler.com.

Chapter 2
Depths of Discovery

<u>Introduction:</u>

Elaine Lemon's "Depths of Discovery" focuses on the power of healing in order to discover our true potential and desires. The process of discovery allows us to honor the sacredness of our pain and suffering. As we listen to our feelings and learn to embrace all the parts of self, we can access the body's innate knowing of our wholeness and well-being. By delving into the depths of our pain we transform our lives through the rediscovery of our wholeness and connect to our deepest desires.

> *"She let go of the shame and the guilt. Seeing that she couldn't have become who she was without those past mistakes. It was time to honor them and thank them, and know that they were some of the best parts of her."*
>
> *~Terri St. Cloud*
> *bonesigharts.com*

Healing empowers us to find our inner strength and life force energy to become unified. Through honoring the sacredness of our pain and suffering, it paves the path of our awareness and growth. Healing is a continuous process of discovery. Integration of the parts of us that we have previously alienated, judged or not accepted; allows us to access more power and joy. Our inner essence is yearning for harmony where we can effortlessly connect to the subtle rhythms of our stillness.

As we listen to our feelings and learn to embrace all parts of self, we access the body's innate knowing of our wholeness and well-being. The destructive parts of us have a message. By delving into the depths of our shadows, we transform our lives through the rediscovery of our wholeness and connect to our deepest desires.

Healing is more than alleviating a symptom. It's a deep, introspective realignment to the process of moving forward. It is an opportunity for us to discover a complete sense of purpose through the alignment of the physical, emotional, mental and spiritual aspects of our lives.

Healing requires active participation. It's the process of discovering the primary reasons for illness, suffering, and disharmony that result in our disconnection from our divine essence. Healing is an opportunity to recognize our inherent wholeness that is always present.

It is during a crisis that we usually come to the point where we must stop and take a deep look into our reality. Crisis provides an opportunity to discover what is most important in life. In the state of suffering, a window is open for us to experience self-reflection.

We are forced to create more integration by leaning into the natural order and flow of life. This is difficult when we have been used to living our lives in a structured way. Our rigidity makes it burdensome to really release blocked emotions.

When we do lean into the healing process, the gift on the other side is a deep feeling of accomplishment. We learn to remove the blocks that prevent us from being whole and connect to a deeper level, where our innate intelligence lies. Leaning into the healing process through connection to the natural order and rhythm of life is the key. Life constantly provides opportunities for growth.

We can choose to take the path of ease and allow it to be effortless or we can resist, and make the process difficult. Our failure to let go of what we think we deserve is what keeps us bound to the cycles of despair and loss.

Resolution comes through our adaptability. Letting go of the parts of us that are not in alignment with our true self allows us to embrace awareness. When we get stuck in perspective and feel that there is only one solution, it stifles our ability to create movement or change. Change will perpetuate a state of fear. Life is not the way it used to be. We often fear the future, resulting in panic that sabotages our healing process.

There are different stages of progress that allow us to overcome the barriers that inhibit us. Through this process, we develop a deeper awareness of who we are. Until we move through each of these stages, we will be bound by the patterns of behavior that stifle our growth.

Loneliness is a common feeling while in the state of transformation and change. It is a belief that we are separate from others. Loneliness is a state of transition between stages. As we let go of one aspect of our lives a state of emptiness occurs. Relaxing into the stillness and peace and embracing the sense of freedom creates a new perceptive.

Emptiness is like a vacuum that attracts more of what we focus our energy on. It is a state of readiness and receptivity of any possible outcome we desire. The energy we focus on draws the experience to us.

We can have a state of aliveness in our life by opening pathways for our growth and expression. As we expand and embrace our true selves, we consciously choose to draw to us the things that bring us the most fulfillment in life.

Now is the time to embody your full capacity by releasing your limitations. An aware state of being awakens the part of you that can experience more than you ever dreamed possible. You can live in a space of empowerment and magnetize your optimal state of well-being.

The Gift of Crisis

Moments of crises humble us and bring us to the core of our being. In the heart of suffering, we are forced to evaluate what matters most. It is the place where you must look hard at what lesson is to be learned, resolved and transformed.

In the state of a crisis, we are forced to look at our true nature as spiritual beings. We have no choice but to go through and explore the dark side of the soul. As one emerges from this space, you are no longer the same person and you are unable to live life as you have previously lived.

Suffering is different from pain. Pain is a discomfort on a physical, emotional, mental or spiritual level, while suffering is an alienation from our true selves. In the act of alienation, we allow for a dishonoring of self. This distorted view is based on a process of numbing and denying our true feelings.

During suffering, we feel a great despair and are unable to get out of the situation. We feels stuck, helpless and paralyzed. We become obsessed with resolving our conflict. When you are in this cycle, you feel rigid and unable to change.

It is important in a state of suffering to let go of the identity we have created that continually avoids our deep self reflection. Exploring within is what is needed for resolution. Healing ourselves from suffering is dependent upon changing our perspectives. It is a time to dig deep within and discover the wisdom of our true selves.

The only way to make it through the suffering is to be with it. You must allow the rhythm to pulse through you and truly connect to the feeling you have denied for so long.

Resistance intensifies the suffering. To deeply heal, one must come to a place of acceptance. Allow yourself to realize that nothing is working right now. The act of yielding to the emotion is key, in order to allow the suffering to shift.

Learning to accept and be in the moment no matter how uncomfortable it is creates movement. However, feeling a separation of self from the whole is the source of the problem. The more accepting and compassionate you are about the parts of you that feel separated, the faster your recovery can begin. In order for you to make progress in your healing, you must pay attention to what your body wants to share.

Others experiences allow us to recognize patterns we have played out in our own lives. Throughout this chapter stories are shared from those who have challenged their darkness. Their awareness inspires us to heal by recognizing and consciously shifting perspective.

She had been sexually abused at an early age. The shame and rage welled inside of her. She was desperately seeking to keep it a secret and just get over it by denying the feelings that constantly wanted to speak through her. She couldn't make the memories go away. Feelings festered within her and grew, eventually manifesting severe gynecological problems. She sought to remove the damaged parts of her body through surgery thinking that this was the answer, but it only magnified the issue.

She judged herself as being wrong and scarred. She felt those parts of her were shameful and wanted to destroy the memories that she continually sought to numb. The intensity only grew.

She could not find peace until she realized that the voice of disharmony deep within needed to be heard. She learned that the part of her that had been wounded was still alive and felt separate from the whole.

With compassion and love, she allowed the abused child within to speak. She moved through the agony, the shame, the resentment and disgust she had for her own body. She trembled as she let the trauma erupt that she had held in for so long. She was no longer willing to deny the pain.

Bringing the story to her consciousness allowed her to recognize all the judgment she held about herself. She was able to look at herself in the mirror again. She trusted and leaned into the process of healing. She accepted the flowing tears that had been stifled for a lifetime.

For the first time, she learned to trust herself and those who gave her the support to move through the process. The part of her that had been harmed could now come home and merge with the whole. She finally found love for the woman who had been repeatedly persecuted by the secret.

Through the long journey of acceptance she discovered compassion for herself. She no longer needed to deny the hurtful parts that had been buried. She found the gift of the trauma by leaning in and discovering she is a strong, courageous woman.

She learned that she deserved to be nurtured, loved and respected, and emerged with a new power and love for herself. She honored her courage to bravely bring her pain to her awareness. In this light of consciousness, she was free.

When we judge our previous experiences, it creates a sense of separation from ourselves. The healing process allows you to lovingly accept and nurture yourself. Your body has messages it desires to share that are an important part of your evolution. Healing beliefs about your experiences is the key to creating change.

Exercise One:

1. Find a place to relax where you will not be disturbed.

2. Begin to breathe in long rhythmic inhales and exhales.
3. Think of a time you have been dishonored and felt deeply separated from yourself. Allow any emotions you feel to come forward and express themselves.

4. Become aware of where you feel tension in your body as you continue to breathe. Focus your breath on the places holding the most tension. Think of the first color that comes to your mind. Breathe that color into that place in your body that is holding the tension.

5. Continuing your breathing, enhance the feeling of separation and despair. What are the emotions that come up in the process?

6. What conclusions did you make about the situation in your state of suffering? What is the self-talk you are repeating?

7. Keep breathing. Bring to your awareness the feeling that nothing is working for you right now. How does this feel?

The Wisdom of Our True Self

The mind and body are inseparable, as diseases will manifest in any and all parts of us that have been ignored. The part of the body holding a memory will demand the attention eventually. Numbing and denying the reality of our stories keeps the wounded part of us alienated.

Awakening is usually the result of a personal crisis. We find that in searching for answers, we must discover the core of the problem of our suffering, or we will always feel there is something deeply missing in our lives. It is important to come to terms with our patterns, unresolved memories, and feelings.

There are many people that desire to stay in their comfort zones and hide behind the illusions they create for themselves. However, daring to go beyond the familiar and venture into the unknown is where possibilities and changes begin. We must break the boundaries, etiquette, and rules that do not resonate as our truth.

He was frozen in his progression. As a well-educated man he had a deep sense of wisdom. Words he spoke inspired others to grow and seize opportunities. However, he wasted much of his time playing video games. He didn't work. He had no desire to. He would rather be poor than take responsibility. He needed to control every situation he experienced. He didn't engage in life.

Those that loved him continually presented opportunities, jobs, and people to connect with. He was emotionally flat and nothing peaked his interest. He never made progress or accomplished anything.

He reluctantly agreed to try healing work only to appease others, although he expected no results. He was aloof and went through the routine but was completely detached.

He was frail and had no vitality. Though no signs of depression were present, there were also no signs of enjoyment either. His body could no longer hold the suppression. Callously, he shared a story about his best friend's wedding.

He had gone to Hawaii to be there for his friend, who was a tower of inspiration for him. They had been good friends for several years. The bachelor party was the day before the wedding. The men attending the pre-wedding event had decided to take a swim in the ocean following the party.

Suddenly large waves appeared where moments before it was calm. He watched in horror as his friends were engulfed in the waves. Knowing that he was the best swimmer there, he heroically swam to the rescue.

He pulled in one friend, laid him on the beach, resuscitated him and jumped back in for another. He repeatedly saved his friends one at a time. He was frantic but he knew he could find the strength to rescue those he cared for so much.

He had brought three people to safety when he discovered the groom, his best friend, was not there. He knew he no longer had energy and strength to make it if he attempted another swim. He could only catch his breath as he watched the escalating waves violently crashing against the beach.

He saw his best friend, face down, floating out in the water. He had not seen him come up for a breath for some time. The waves slowly brought the lifeless body close enough to the shore that the gathering crowd could help him to safety.

The paramedics arrived and were trying to bring the groom back. He felt, now there was help, that everything would be okay.

He waited in the hospital for what felt like an eternity. Finally, the doctor arrived delivering the news that his best friend did not survive. He didn't know how to react; it was all too surreal and tragic. As the best man, he had to tell the bride to be that there would be no wedding.

He realized at the moment of sharing this story that he could never trust the Higher Powers to support him. He had put in all his effort to save his friends to no avail. How could he find faith in anything?

He had not experienced emotions stir within him ever since the incident. Now tears flooded and he revealed the pain he had held within. He now recognized the belief he made at the time of the tragedy. If he did not put effort into any endeavor, he would not be disappointed by the outcome. With all of his heart he wanted his friend to live. When his best friend died, a part of him did too.

Knowing he did not have the tenacity to bear disappointment again, he shut down his emotions. He designed a life that would never bring disappointment. He also experienced no joy.

Through small steps he was able forgive himself and learn that every person has their unique life path. Though he does not understand why his friend had to die, he learned that he could trust that everything has its own rhythm and timing. It was time for his friend to pass on.

He chose to lean in and trust life again. He challenged himself to embrace opportunities that were presented to him. In his renewed zest for life, he forgave himself and discovered that life has amazing opportunities if one is fully willing to engage.

Our soul's longing to heal directs us to where we are holding trapped fear. Fear can be on a physical, emotional, mental or spiritual level. We must challenge these obstacles and look at the limiting beliefs we hold. Shining the light of awareness on the problem is the key to resolution.

It is important to clear past emotions and memories of incidents that we believe keep us small. This energy, when redirected, allows us to receive full empowerment and wholeness. Then we are able to use the energy to create integrity, clarity and purpose.

Personal healing requires time to withdraw, go inward, and take notice of your sensitivity. You must learn to accept all that has happened to you while releasing your judgment. You are the creator of your experiences and on some level you have attracted this opportunity of learning for your self discovery.

We must unravel and heal from not only our personal wounds, but also the collective wounds of society. Look deeply at the holding patterns and limitations you have set for yourself. Perhaps you have thought that an issue is too deep to heal or too overwhelming.

The Doorway to Discovery

Feelings previously not felt, ignored, or denied are the pathways to the discovery of your true self. Even if you feel you have dealt with an issue before, be aware that we are in a spiral path of healing. There are times we have to revisit our old issues several times in order to fully understand the core of the problem and find resolution.

Traveling through the emotions allows a sense of empowerment to emerge. It builds a foundation based on clarity, intuition, and discernment.

Our greatest fear is death. If you follow your emotion to the core, the fear of dying will be the issue. When you clear and transform your cellular memory through allowing issues to arise to the surface, the body can manifest its divine blueprint.

Instead of escaping a feeling that is miserable, simply be with it. Enhance the feeling until it becomes unbearable. In this space, observe your reactions and emotions. Enhancing the feeling of intensity, free of judgment, allows the body to experience it on a fuller level. The only way out of a problem is to go through it.

Exercise 2:

1. Go to a place where you are all alone and will not be disturbed.

2. Stand in the middle of the floor and begin to rhythmically breathe. Inhale and exhale. Become very present of your physical body.

3. Reach down on the ground and draw a circle that represents a sacred space for you. Step in the circle and sit in the space.

4. Take 3 deep breaths, fully inhaling and exhaling.

5. Think of your greatest fear. Focus on any experiences you have had with this fear. Ask yourself if this is an experience that has happened to you or something you are afraid of in the future.

7. Feel yourself melt deeply into the fear. You are safe in your sacred space. Go inward and notice what emotions the fear brings up for you.

8. Ask yourself what crisis is attached to the fear. How old do you feel you were when you connect to the fear?

9. What is your judgment of yourself when you feel this fear?

10. Follow the fear to the worst case scenario. If your greatest fear happened, how would you feel? Keep asking the question and allow your inner knowing to respond.

11. What is the overall feeling after following the emotion? Did challenging the fear assist to transform the feeling to a state of peace?

12. Thank your fear for speaking to you and close your sacred space. Record what you felt.

Perspective or True Identity

Gratitude for what the experience is teaching you provides the energy to transform. Your suffering is the doorway to your desires. Moving through the magnitude of the feeling creates a turning point in your life. You can release the bondage of your old identity and create a bridge to the remembrance of your power.

She spent half of her life with a man that didn't notice or acknowledge her. Though she was beautiful, she never knew it. She thought her attractiveness was gone after bearing children. He never made her feel special.

She began to wither inside. She was hungry and desirous to have someone notice her, compliment her, and nurture her. She knew if she didn't leave him, she would not have the strength to live. She had lost all the passion in her life. Finally she chose to leave him.

Naively she imagined that she would simply find a companion that loved her the way she desired. To her despair, she continued to attract partners that didn't see her talents or cherish her radiant spirit. They disregarded her dreams and neglected her longing for connection.

The men she dated always had something more important than her. She knew what she desired and deserved but she was unable to change the pattern that, hauntingly, was her reality. She did not attract men that saw who she was or desired to support her.

The depths of pain from the loneliness became her familiar friend and greatest teacher. She surrendered to the pattern she was living and chose to look within to find resolution. She was not willing to go through another round of neglect with a relationship that left her longing for fulfillment.

In the solitude of the silence she recognized that she must find forgiveness not only for her partners but most importantly for herself. She had never seen her own value. How could anyone else? She had felt she was only important when she supported another to succeed. She had never taken a stand for herself.

Guided by her internal wisdom, she found the peace in her loneliness. She began to acknowledge her own needs and gained the power and strength to live her passion. She remembered her beauty that had always been present. She stood strong in her wholeness and she flourished.

She blessed the despair and thanked it for the journey of awakening. Stepping into her sense of empowerment, she created a space for a relationship that would cherish her.

Remembering Our Wholeness

Our stories teach us to become aware of our desires and find a way to achieve them. We do this by merging our darkness or shadow into the light. In essence, we allow the part of us that has been separate to come home.

We must learn to honor ourselves and face the experience of distress. As we recognize the importance of going back and viewing our time of struggle, we can integrate the experience.

An important part of the healing process is to realize that we do not want the experience anymore. You must confront the feeling that was behind the struggle, take accountability for the pattern, and discover it doesn't have power over you any longer.

When we are stuck in perspective, we cannot embrace our true identity. Changing our viewpoint often brings a level of chaos. Chaos is energy that teaches us to discover steps for growth and development.

Coming to a space of acceptance of the chaos allows the anger towards yourself and the situation to be replaced with self-respect. This process allows you to gain the tools that you need to reclaim who you really are.

As we take back our personal power, forgiveness sets us free. We must honor ourselves as unified beings and remember our wholeness.

The universe is continually expanding. In order for us to align with this frequency, we must invariably cultivate our evolution and redefine who we are. Our soul wants us to reach our highest potential.

Love of our purpose is the force that creates passion. Passion is what fuels us to expand and reach for our fullest possibilities. With passion, we discover the gift of change and embrace our growth. Learning to say yes to life through creativity, growth, and expression allows us to face our challenges and put love into action.

Experiencing the taste of success deepens our faith and encourages us to move forward. Openness and willingness to reclaim our highest potential comes from the core of our hearts. We can create conviction by being in integrity from within.

We must pursue the desires that our soul yearns for. There is a treasure in every circumstance that serves us by building a solid foundation for our aspirations. Follow the path that easily opens and makes you feel more alive.

Exercise 3:

1. Go to a place where you can lay down and not be disturbed.

2. Turn off the lights and sit in the darkness. Begin to breathe deeply.

3. What is the crisis you have not wanted to deal with? Explore the story, allowing it play out in your mind.

4. What perspective do you have about the situation? Do you feel like a victim? Do you feel betrayed? Perhaps it is a feeling of helplessness, insignificance or pointlessness? Allow the perspective to be present while you continue to breathe.

5. Notice how you have played this story over and over in your mind. What is the story that keeps you stuck?

6. What chaos do you feel in your life?

7. How does that chaos affect your physical body?

8. Become aware of the darkness around you. What does the darkness represent to you?

9. What does your soul yearn for the most?

10. In the awareness of your perspective, what is keeping you attached to the perspective?

11. What lesson did you learn from looking at your perspective deeply? What is the opposite perspective than the one you have?

Separation from Source

Illness and disease are the body's way of sending the message that you cannot continue the destructive patterns you have previously chosen. Severely suppressive reactions stem from our impressionable childhood, life experiences and our genetics.

The brain is the control center of the body. The brain's main occupation is to keep us alive for the subsequent moment. Our brain is similar to a very powerful computer; specifically programmed for our biological survival.

There is a connection between the parts of the brain that correspond to each organ. When there is a significant stress or imbalance, our body creates a compensation process where one system borrows energy from another.

Our moods are affected by conflict and are stored in our energy fields. However, if the body is overloaded with stress to the point that it can no longer manage it, the body responds by becoming ill.

In a state of high affliction, lack of adequate recuperation from a conflict creates illness. The body perceives the continued levels of stress as a threat. In response to the imbalance, it triggers its survival program, which causes a disturbance in health.

A dramatic or unexpected shock that results in feelings of isolation, coupled with the constant repetition of thoughts, strongly influences the body's immune response and generates physical symptoms. Thus, emotional disturbances and patterns break down the body's resistance.

The basis for all illness is a deep sense of separation from Source. To truly heal our physical bodies, we must take accountability of our destructive patterns. Being aware of emotional disturbances and learning to give a voice to suppressed issues opens the gateway for true healing to occur.

He had inflammation of his liver. His skin and eyes were yellow with jaundice. His muscles ached and he had lost his appetite. He was always fatigued and felt weak; his liver was increasingly showing signs of damage.

He resented his life but was resistant to change. He felt powerless, angry and full of revenge. His demands from life overloaded him and he felt he was unable to deal with any aspect of life anymore. Deep inside, he had an increasing amount of self-doubt.

His underlying feelings were that he was a bad person and he had no right to live. He was exasperated and felt hopeless to stand up to his wife. Their fighting had perpetuated and his resentment toward her continued to grow. He felt an overwhelming lack of recognition and support.

He had tried to hide the reality that his marriage had severe problems. The feelings of hopelessness and despair were overwhelming. He lacked the psychological strength to take any action.

He became aware that he could not continue on the path he was on. Life had no meaning living this way. He could no longer numb the pain that he felt.

He used the physical sensations that fatigued him to draw himself inward. He intensified the overwhelming anger and despair. He gave himself permission to let his anger be present, physically hitting his bed and releasing deep surges of frustration that erupted. He allowed his anger to be heard.

He had held his rage in long enough. He continued to allow the deep expression of anger about his life and discontentment to be voiced. He no longer had the strength to contain his feelings and became willing to face the reality and move through it.

Overwhelmed with anger and exhaustion, he sat down and surrendered to the sobs of despair. They completely engulfed him. He knew he could no longer live life this way. He had resisted what his inner guidance had been telling him for some time. It was time to end his marriage and move on.

Making the decision to fully embrace his suffering he recognized was making himself sick. He had sought to extinguish his inner truth about the reality that his marriage was irreconcilable.

He moved forward with his divorce and in the process he became aware that in his solitude there was peace. The stillness was his friend. He found comfort in his quiet moments. It gave him energy to nurture himself.

He began to write journals and create an avenue for his negative expression. He followed through with visualizations of his body being healthy and vibrant and focused on the small successes of increased physical activity.

He examined his childhood experiences, finding the source of his pain in events that he previously did not acknowledge. He allowed his frustration to surface as he taught his inner child that he would listen to whatever the wounded part needed to express.

He found the sources that helped him heal. His body was healthy and functioning and he regained his strength.

Being accountable for his attitudes, he was able to create well-being in his life. He learned that his life and his opinions deeply mattered. He was aware that his projections to his wife were his feelings about himself. He realized she was his greatest teacher, for she helped him to discover his value.

He transformed a toxic situation into a new way of being. He learned to love himself and the love changed his vibration to optimal health. He honored himself and found pleasure in the simplicity of life.

Embodied in the darkness of our shadows is the power and wisdom to transform and heal ourselves. Exploring, revealing and releasing our hidden wounds awakens the pathway to our wholeness.

Physical problems are the direct result of our unwillingness to change our course. Preceding an illness, there is usually an experience that invokes the disruptive pattern of health. Through exploring our life events, thoughts, and feelings at the time the symptom manifested on a physical level, we can significantly unravel the healing process.

Power and Wisdom to Heal

We all have distorted aspects of ourselves that we do not want to address. These are subconscious areas that we fear. They hinder us from expressing our true selves, our fulfillment in relationships, our interaction in the social world and the way we relate to others, as well as our spiritual connection.

Awareness is the healing factor in any situation. It brings to the light the dark parts of our shadows; the issues we do not want to remember, that distort and create disturbances in our lives. We must follow the avenues that open us to exploring how we have embraced our separation.

Our bodies are always looking for the familiar. This is why it is so difficult to change our behaviors and attitudes. We have spent a tremendous amount of energy concealing the underlying issues and avoiding the fear of our dark side. As human beings we believe that it is easier to deal with a predictable outcome instead of challenging the situation.

Our bodies are also continually searching for the level of homeostasis where they feel balanced. When issues that are held on the subconscious and super-conscious minds are addressed, it creates chaos. Chaos causes a shift, affecting the body in a significant way and forcing us to discover a new level of balance. In any form of chaos, there is a source of energy available to generate a new experience.

Eliminating the restrictions and burdens that limit our life energy enhances our vitality and empowerment. We can do this simply by releasing our resistance to change. Transforming our breakdowns into breakthroughs allows us to step closer to the true power we have within. Fearlessly approaching chaos not only teaches but also allows us to face the danger.

Evolutionary growth within us brings more light. Since healing is a spiral force, it brings more light to the surface. However, it also brings a deeper level of darkness to the surface in order to heal. Being brave enough to venture into the darkness is where our gifts lie.

Embodied in the darkness is wisdom to empower and transform oneself. Our souls emerge from the darkness, ready to claim our highest potential. We must embrace the expression of our life unfolding. There is a higher order of consciousness we can always attain.

Exercise 4:

1. Find a quiet space where you can be alone.

2. Begin to breathe, deeply inhaling and exhaling. Create a flow in your breath.

3. Focus on your body. What illness or ailment have you continually struggled with? Place your attention on that part of your body.

4. Ask your illness what it wants to communicate to you. What purpose is it playing in your life?

5. How has this illness isolated you from others? Did the isolation bother you or give you relief?

6. What situation happened that was shocking to you just before you got sick?

7. How has the illness kept you from feeling connected to your Source?

8. Really connect with the physical disturbance. Ask the illness what it needs to feel whole again.

9. What course of action have you been unwilling to change in your life?

10. What would allow you to feel more balance?

11. What breakthrough would assist you to feel more powerful?

12. Thank your illness for being a teacher to you. Be with the illness; do not resist it.

Quantum Healing and Change

Human beings have two distinct immune systems. The first system is the physical chemistry and physiology that connects to the encoded parts of their DNA. This defense system plays a role in fighting off infection.

The other immune system is the magnetic or multidimensional energy that is connected to the conscious awareness and spiritual intent. Our thoughts and desires give direction to the DNA which then responds through magnetic transmission, creating more immune cells. Through your intent, you can create quantum healing and change.

The multidimensional layer is dormant and needs to be awakened in order for it to fully function. It is magnetic and is not bound by chemical rules. However, it is more powerful than the body's chemical reactions.

The body is in partnership with our sacred nature. Pure energy work, meditation and spiritual connection allow the body to merge with its inner knowledge of how to heal and alter cellular structure on a quantum level.

He had experienced a scratchy, hoarse throat for some time now. He ignored it, thinking it would go away eventually. Over time it got worse and he was constantly clearing his throat. It became difficult to swallow; his throat was persistently painful and swollen. He also had a bump in his neck but he did not get a doctor's opinion about his condition until he began to have difficulties breathing. He was diagnosed with laryngeal cancer and a surgery date was set immediately.

He had spent many years being unable to speak up for himself out of fear of humiliation and invalidation. In the moment of complete loss of his voice, he was willing to look deeper at all he was trying to suppress.

He had gone through some difficult times with his career that he felt guilt and shame about. He had believed that he deserved to be punished because of what he had put his family through. Because of this experience he had guilt about expressing his own needs, which resulted in feeling invalidated, humiliated and ignored. He was unable to speak his truth. He felt as if he had a tight band around his neck that prevented him from genuine expression.

He was willing to recognize how small he had held himself in the past, a recurring problem for him. By truly looking at the reality of his actions he saw the importance of making changes. He communicated and opened up, expressing what was most important for his nurturance and care.

He expressed to his family the words and messages that he had always wanted to tell them. He recorded stories and advice that he desired to be kept in his history. He wanted to have a remembrance of his spoken words of wisdom and love. He allowed his communication to flow freely.

His surgery date arrived. He was highly aware that he would not be able to speak or communicate after the removal of his larynx. However, he seized his final moments to voice what his heart desired. His willingness to openly express was incredibly healing for him. He had peace and awareness that everything would be okay.

At the time of the surgery the doctor was confused. The previous medical examinations and X-Rays clearly showed the mass on his larynx. However, as the doctor explored the tissue and structure, there was no evidence of any cancer in his body.

The process of allowing his flow of expression where there was once only restriction removed the toxic poisons and illness that could have been had tragic results. What appeared to be a miracle to his doctors and family was a direct result of him creating movement in his larynx when previously there was none.

More powerful than any chemical reaction in the body, is the awareness and spiritual intent that gives direction to healing. Consciousness of his issue allowed him to connect to the quantum healing power of the DNA and changed his physical chemistry.

Our Divine Blueprint

We are designed to be operating and functioning on a complete level of wholeness. Healing and stability takes place when using pure intent or consciousness coupled with energy healing methods. The body has the attributes to cure itself through rejuvenation of our health through its supreme knowing.

The DNA holds the quantum blueprint of your divinity. Both physically and spiritually, DNA is the core element of who we are. It carries the biologically inherited traits in our chemistry. Even more significant are the traits of our personalities carried by the Akashic Record. This is the divine wisdom of your innate wholeness from all multidimensional parts of you.

Our DNA knows what we need to heal and activates various energies through our awareness that create miraculous changes in our physical bodies. It orchestrates and aligns the synchronicity through the magnetism of our cellular structure.

Exercise 5:

1. Find an isolated space where you can deeply meditate. Perhaps it is in the mountains, ocean or by a river. Find a place that helps you feel alive and connected to nature.

2. Begin rhythmically breathing. Focus on going inward to your heart.

3. When you are fully connected to your heart, continuing breathing deeply. Feel how each breath feeds every cell in your body.

4. Inhale and take in the beautiful nature that surrounds you.

5. Exhale and release any resistance, feelings of frustration, or experiences that keep you from fully experiencing this moment.

6. Feel the expansion of your heart's energy receiving the beautiful nature around you.

7. Allow your heart to connect with your Spiritual Source. Bring in the golden light of the divine love. Allow your heart to receive the energy.

8. Continue expanding your heart and allow it to be filled with gratitude for this moment.

9. Visualize your DNA receiving the messages of love from your heart and Source.

10. Merge with the knowledge that you are deeply loved. You can be healed. You have all the capacity within you.

11. Continue taking in the life force energy in the space of gratitude and love for this moment.

DNA activation and cellular healing can be accelerated through energy and support from a healer that understands the process. You may want to consider using someone that can give you the extra energy you need to accelerate your healing journey.

Compassionately Nurture and Love Ourselves

Have you ever noticed that when you are doing well with the achievement a goal, there comes a time when you sabotage your efforts and do something that creates the disharmony again?

We have a part of us that actually desires pain and self-destruction. When this is triggered we are connected to previous events. There is payoff we receive that beckons us to stay in a familiar pattern.

Even when an issue has been healed, you may need to revisit the situation to heal a deeper level of attachment. It is important for imbalances to be brought to your awareness, and cleared.

Recognizing her pattern of self destruction, she directly challenges her thought. She has repeatedly gone back to her addictions to cover the pain that speaks through her. Years of disappointment and frustration beckon her to suppress the pain just one more time. She has come too far to trust the yearnings that beckon her to come back to her eminent need to feed her addiction.

In this moment, she reminds the unhealed part of her that feeding her addiction does not make the feeling go away permanently. It is merely a band-aid that perpetuates the problem. The longing subsides when she allows the truth to be spoken to her soul.

Facing the irrational chaos, she listens to her inner knowing and permits the feeling to momentarily fester and grow. Going to the edge of the discomfort coupled with her determination to heal, she merges with the source of her suffering that had frightened her so much. She bursts into tears, releasing the storm that brewed within her.

She is no longer willing to shut out the pain. She has given the pain permission to have a voice and share the darkness that it had hidden for so long. It erupts from within like a volcano, allowing its eminence to be ever present. Her breakthrough gives her the energy to generate power and strength.

She breathes in the golden light of healing and releases the pain through her exhalation. She has created space for the light and in that space, she remembers that the only way out of the problem is to move through it.

One of the best ways to deal with sabotage, self-destruction, and obstacles that take you away from your goal or intent is to ask yourself what payoff you are actually receiving. Perhaps you hold the belief that you get sympathy, or that you are able to the control events in some way.

Even though it does not make sense to the conscious mind, there are subconscious and super-conscious aspects that play out these roles in an endless loop, as if it is a game. It will continue until we bring the emotion to the surface. It is similar to a child having a tantrum because it's not getting its needs met.

When you notice these patterns of self-destruction recurring, have compassion and be free of judgment for yourself. You must lovingly nurture yourself, similar to how you would nurture your own child.

Our parents did the best they could with the tools that they had to care for us. However, because of the lack of love and healing they had for themselves, they were never really able to fulfill our needs.

Through observation you will discover there is an immature inner child that has been wounded and hasn't grown up with the rest of you. It is important to allow the fragmented aspect of yourself to let go of the distress and grow through your adult perspective.

The majority of our beliefs are made through vulnerable experiences of our childhood. We tend to recreate the neglect in our own lives because it feels familiar; it is something we are use to. The inner child is creating the disturbance to heal.

Unresolved issues from the past and present, and the fear of the future create imbalance and lack of harmony. Nearly all physical issues stem from not dealing with deep-seated feelings that are the source of disturbance.

Deep within you know you deserve much more. However, you continually settle because you do not trust your inner knowledge. There is a gift behind each experience. Discovering the gift allows the separated part of you to unite with your whole self.

Magnify the Issue

Use physical pain to draw yourself in and magnify the issue. The objective is to allow the pain trapped in your system to surface. Ask the pain what it wants to teach you. What does the pain stop you from doing? What would you be doing if you didn't have the pain?

Our pain is not our enemy. Our pain is a wakeup call to look deeply at the direction you are going in your life. Your body can show you the areas where we need to have forgiveness and compassion for yourself. In a world that focuses on instant relief to make the symptoms go away, we are missing the opportunity to heal the underlying issues that take us through our evolution. Continually avoiding and suppressing the stories that need to be explored causes the issue to go deeper and grow into a bigger problem.

Until you connect with the story the pain is holding, whether it is physical, emotional, mental or spiritual pain, there can be no resolution. You must challenge your illusions in order to truly heal.

Behind every experience that takes away our power, annihilates our relationships and deteriorates our health, is fear. Challenging the reality of the fear allows us to identify the worst case scenario. We can then eliminate the anticipation of the situation.

Pursue the Path of Light

We can disempower the illusion by merging with it. Merging refers to asking the alienated parts of self to work as a unit. Uniting our wounded parts creates a space where the power of fear is no longer an issue, opening a new relationship and perspective with self.

Dedication to healing takes recognition of the importance of doing whatever it takes to grow and shed limiting beliefs. Pain gives us an opportunity to become aware of all of our experiences and learn to respect them, regardless of the stories of the past. We must invite all parts of us to participate with the whole again.

You are afraid of pain because you fear it will destroy you. It will. It destroys your resistance, shifts your identity and takes off the masks of your illusions. Movement shines light on who you really are.

Fear does not respect the boundaries you have created. You must break the rigidities you have created. Delving into the fear allows you to experience the spontaneous, wild freedom that connects you to your aliveness.

We open space by releasing the density. Our well-being is dependent upon clearing old patterns, memories, and past emotions.

Overtime you will learn to observe the pain and drama without identifying and attaching it to the suffering. The inner space of stillness is where peace will reside.

She daringly left an abusive relationship where she had experienced emotional neglect and despair. She was brave and strong, seeking to instill stability and well-being for her children. Her ex-husband did not make it easy for her, as he insisted that she must be punished for taking a stand for her life and taking her children away from a painful environment.

Her pain intensified throughout her body. The fibromyalgia and desire to find relief from the pain consumed her focus. All of her money went towards finding solutions while her pain made it increasingly difficult to continue working. In the middle of her struggle, her ex-decided to quit paying her the alimony he owed. She had no choice but to fight a long battle with him in court.

Slowy, she let go of all her physical possessions. She lost her home, and let go of the things that she once thought had very much value and meaning to her. She surrendered to the flow and trusted that if she followed the path of light, a doorway would open.

She faced the overwhelming disillusion of loss and discovered in the midst of releasing her attachments to things, that she and her family were always okay. Earth angels were there to care for her needs and help her in her time of tragedy.

Her pain held the secrets of her past. She was no longer willing to be bullied by the men of the past. She had allowed men to treat her bad her whole life. She now reclaimed her power and strongly held a place for her own respect and her body began to heal.

In the space of loss, she discovered the true source of her strength and power. She learned that material possessions only support the illusion that joy comes from outside of her. She recognized that her real beauty is in the power of surrender and allowing miracles to occur.

You must consistently venture into the darkness, where you judge yourself in order reclaim your power. This is the key to well being. Life is teaching us to say yes to our passions, creativity, service, and growth. Our deepest desire is to claim a true expression of self.

Pursue the path of light, the longing in the heart, where ease effortlessly unfolds. Your life is waiting patiently for you to follow and act upon your inner dreams.

Exercise 6:

1. Write down a time you can remember that you made a goal and you were doing well achieving it.

2. Recall something you did to sabotage your goal after you had been doing so well.

3. What event occurred to trigger the response to make the decision your goal was no longer important?

4. What was the payoff you received from disregarding your goal?

5. Has this issue happened before? Have you had to revisit the issue many times?

6. How does your inner child respond when it has a tantrum? Do you get angry? Do you scream? Do you cry? Do you withdraw? Notice how old you feel when you have this tantrum.

7. Now close your eyes, and begin to breath. Focus on what you look like as child. Notice your eyes. Let the adult you look deeply in the eyes of the inner child. Open your heart and feel the inner child's fear.

8. How can you lovingly nurture your inner child?

9. What story does the child want you to know? What kind of pain is he or she still holding?

10. Let your inner child feel your heart overflow with love towards him or her.

11. Ask your inner child to move from the outside of you and merge inside.

12. Let your inner child know that you are aware that he or she is still there. It is safe for him or her to be with you. They will be protected from now on.

13. Continue to breathe and feel the warmth and unity of the connection.

Accessing Our Purpose and Talents

All of our rigid thought forms, structured beliefs and rules we have repeated in our lifetimes create neurological pathways in our brain. Our bodies then take the incoming emotion, thought, or energy of these patterns and guide the new experiences to the familiar pathway.

The way to connect with the original healthy pathway is to assume total responsibility for the issue, make it conscious and then connect to the power of infinite love within.

Being responsible means healing all parts of the self. We embrace our denial. We forgive our judgments. Our betrayal becomes trust. We reunite with abandonment and surrender to our isolation. Self-accountability creates our deepest healing.

Until we delve deeply into our issues of personality, we will often find that our purpose and talents are inaccessible. To truly be able to utilize your greatest power, you must dissolve beliefs and become conscious of the structures you are holding.

There are four stages of expansion that we as humans must explore and resolve in order to really create the lives we desire. We create deep programs that keep us bound by a continuous feedback through our decisions and patterns of behavior.

You can move through each of these stages by approaching them through self-introspection and connection to your higher light. In addition, a healer that understands these stages can help you to move through them.

Failure Stage:

The failure stage is when you have no motivation, drive nor vitality to achieve anything in life. You have little faith in your abilities for accomplishment. You experience too much defeat and thus your resistance creates obstacles to the completion of projects. We tend to focus on how unfair life is. Some of us feel life is cruel and can resort to drugs and alcohol abuse in order to suppress our deficiency.

Shame, guilt and blame are the common in this stage, and in a state of lethargy, there are no signs of progress. In the Failure Stage, we constantly have bad luck and feel a force of resistance in everything we do.

Helpless Stage:

In the helpless stage we feel stuck in our situation. Relationships and jobs are unfulfilling. We feel we do deserve love or recognition.

We can get aroused and excited about doing something but they never really try to accomplish it. We cannot concentrate, and become irritated by small obstacles.

Feeling anxiety, smothered, depressed and desperate are all common emotions within this phase. We acknowledge the possibility to accomplish something but it just never happens.

Determination Stage:

The determination stage is where we know we will receive our desires. Even if there is resistance, approaching a situation with certainty, we feel we will move through the circumstance and receive our desired result.

Throughout this stage, we consistently work hard and usually achieve reasonable success. However, we have to put in a steady effort; despite not being the most talented in an area, we know that if persistent, we can secure success and receive our full desires for our effort.

Freedom Stage:

The freedom stage is where we receive success easily. Things come to us readily. People are attracted to us in this stage and tend to want to help. People approach those who are open to receiving their desires. We effortlessly attract our sole purpose and it becomes easy to get what we want.

There is no underlying resistance and nothing needs to be forced. Grace now permeates our life, allowing us to receive much more than we ever imagined possible.

One can easily move through these stages as we let go of the resistance, break down the barriers of belief in limitations and surrender to the inner guidance that assists to navigate our path.

All of her life she felt she couldn't accomplish anything. She didn't even dare to try. She was insecure and self focused, knowing that she would fail at anything she attempted. It was safest for her to stay isolated and invisible.

She saw no value in her life. She viewed life as a game of survival. She felt much shame and guilt for never doing anything significant. She observed others' ambitions and was discouraged because others seemed to thrive. She felt life was so unfair.

She was the victim in most areas of her life. She had experienced a very difficult childhood and didn't feel like she could ever recover enough to be able to make any contribution to anything. She would forever be stuck in her pattern of despair and uselessness.

There was someone that saw more inside of her than she did. He showed her opportunities and challenged her to take small steps towards a goal. She cautiously began to explore the small areas of passion she had.

Still, she felt that life was unfulfilling. The yearnings from within seemed like fantasies to her. They mockingly reminded her of all she could never have. The feelings of being stuck were unbearable. She didn't believe she deserved much so she easily settled. She didn't feel her needs or wants could be met.

She experienced depression, suicidal thoughts, feelings of escaping and desperation. She had little hope that anything could help her get better. Most of the efforts she made didn't seem to give her much in return.

In a state of complete despair, she decided to get some healing work. She began to look at her beliefs and discovered that she was creating the reality that she lived. Her constant thoughts of negativity and despair perpetuated the situation. She discovered that the more she hated her position, the more stuck she was.

She began to find compassion and love for her journey. She was learning valuable lessons about her experiences in life. She discovered that she is not the victim and began to take accountability for her situation.

Her learning was difficult but she could now see some light at the end of the tunnel. She was determined to try to heal. She became encouraged. She knew that even though she was not the most talented at something, her continued effort would create progress.

She became aware of new patterns emerging. Her old ways of seeing the world had shifted. The underlying resistance was gone. She began to discover that in this space, things came to her easier.

She no longer forced life to happen, but allowed grace to dictate her progression. She evaluated her beliefs deeper. She discovered that she didn't really need anything. Breakthroughs occurred easily as she let go of the limitations that had previously held her prisoner.

She began to attract her desires easily now. Opportunities were presented to her that she never imagined possible. She discovered her strength and support from all areas in her life. She realized her outer world is simply a reflection of her inner world.

In this space, she chose love and love radiated back to her.

Our mind is powerful. It seeks to control everything based on previous experience. It is important to realize that if you desire to have a different outcome, you must do things differently than you have in the past.

Our Outer World is a Reflection of Our Inner World

Your outer world is simply a reflection of your inner world. Everything you experience is a mirror of the energy you hold about yourself. Your relationships, careers, and ability to manifest your desires are a gauge of what is occurring within.

The only way to change your experience is to take responsibility for thoughts, feelings, beliefs, and projections. You must look deeply at all denial, judgments, isolation, and feelings of betrayal.

Love is what allows you the freedom to experience life the way you desire. Love begins within in you. Nurturing the tender seeds of love for yourself allows you to receive what you want easily and effortlessly.

Exercise 7:

1. What is a rigid thought form you have had that has kept you stuck in a stage of growth?

2. Think of something you would really like to achieve. What stage of expansion are you currently experiencing?

3. How does the stage feel to you?

4. Instead of resisting and resenting the stage you are experiencing, how can you be at peace with it?

5. What step will help you move closer to your truest desire?

6. How do your current experiences in your life and outer world reflect how you feel inside?

7. What are your inner feelings?
8. What is one step you can take to find more compassion and love for yourself?

Growth and Expression

Abundance is manifesting optimal health and fulfillment in all areas of our lives. Embracing our truest desires opens an avenue to fulfill our needs. We can enhance our ability to live our best life by gathering tools and support systems. Growth and expression open the doorways to living life to its fullest.

There are only two processes that occur in any system. There is a regeneration process that focuses on healing, expansion, growth, and learning. The other process is degeneration where there is a breakdown of a system resulting in contraction, deterioration, elimination and death.

We are either expanding or contracting. Every aspect of life goes through these two phases. If you are not experiencing growth in any area, you are dying. You cannot stay stationary.

Following the healing process, we can embrace the state of expansion by focusing on the times we have had success. It is important to forgive your past and change the course of your future.

Light is the source that gives us more information. Darkness is where we are being misinformed and information is being withheld. Our positive beliefs draw to us expansion in thoughts, ideas, health and well-being. Our focus on negative beliefs and previous mishaps leads us to deterioration and destructive outcomes.

Every belief has a polar opposite that you have not manifested. If your belief system has focused on the negative spiral, you can consciously choose to have the opposite experience. The only battle that exists between light and dark is the one that occurs within.

Visualizations Change Our Reality

Our powerful imaginations can change our reality through the visualization processes. After the exploration of the traumas and darkness you can reconstruct your history. Childhood memories and other pain can be rewritten by envisioning a different outcome.

Taking the attention away from the negative experiences and redirecting the energy towards positive visualizations creates integration. Feeling and experiencing a positive emotion in a loving way shifts our entire chemical makeup and changes the vibration we are feeling.

Lovingly and supportively realize that all of your experiences have led you to the lessons of growth that have built a foundation for you to thrive. You do not know what you want until you know what we don't want.

Use your negative experiences as a catalyst to push you to fulfillment; they have illuminated the most important aspects of your life that you desire to embrace. Your fear serves you because it holds the keys to alchemy and your evolution. Through rising above the boundary that has been your reality, you can experience more joy than you ever imagined.

Our emotions are powerful in their creative capacities. Follow the avenue that opens and allows the light and joy to overflow. Trusting our deepest wisdom leads us to opportunities that shed light on the path of true happiness.

Energy is like the ocean. It moves in waves of ebb and flow. Life has a natural cycle. Embrace life's rhythm and natural flow. Life is cyclical and flows in phases of expansion and contraction. Life is a spiral and we pass through stages over and over to gain a higher perspective of our reality.

Every experience you have had is an opportunity to gain greater clarity, vision and power. You can make every area in your life thrive as you align to your divine purpose and blueprint.

When you truly accept the lessons, grow and gain compassion for our experiences, you will no longer have to experience the pain. Living life in a way that demonstrates your trust in your destiny is the only way you can affect your future.

Life is intended to come together effortlessly. When you are on your path of awakening, synchronicity occurs easily. The natural order brings us to alignment with the people and situations that continue our evolution and growth.

The frequency of love and the connection to light, which is information, is the basis of all creation. All our experiences have prepared us to achieve our desires through changing our vibration. A state of receptivity comes from being in the space of love.

Honor your deepest desires. They are showing you the direction to live life to its fullest. As you experience more of what you love, life becomes fulfilling and happy. Success comes from loving what you have and what you are experiencing. This creates expansion by bringing in more life.

Where you direct your energy is what you will have. If you dislike something you will be stuck with it. We cannot release any experience until we learn to love it and learn from the experience. Once we truly love something we can set it free.

Exercise 8:

1. Find a quiet place where you will not be disturbed. Begin to breathe; inhale and exhale in perfect rhythm.

2. Focus on the abundance you desire in your life. What is the optimal fulfillment you could have in your relationships, health, fiancial freedom, leisure, and spiritual growth?

3. Go through each area of your life and breath energy into the most fulfilling experiences you can imagine.

4. Notice as you focus positive energy, you are in the flow of regeneration and growth. You feel more alive and desire to expand.

5. Redirect the energy to the opposite. Become aware of how quickly you can begin to take the downward spiral. This exercise is to remind you of the importance of feeding positive thoughts.

6. Now return to the optimal experience that brings passion to your life. Breath in golden light and feel it flood over the top of your head, down to your third eye, breathe through your throat, and expand it in your chest. Continue to breathe the golden light through you abdomen, pelvis and then out through your feet, connecting to the earth.

7. Observe how everything you desire opens up for you.

8. What would it be like to always have this bliss in your life? You CAN live a life free of pain. Breathe that feeling throughout your whole body. Allow it to move through your feet. Plant yourself firmly on the ground connecting to the energy of Mother Earth. Feel the support of the Divine Mother pulse back through you.

9. Continue to be in this space of bliss. This is your birthright. In this space you are completely aligned with all you deserve.

10. Take a picture of this moment with your mind. Place it in your hands and hold your hands over your heart. Breath in the energy in remembrance of the feeling of bliss.

Life Force Energy

One of our greatest desires is to achieve success while making a contribution to the whole. We have a sense from within of what we can truly be when we are not restricted by the many limitations and barriers we create. This motivates us to reach for our dreams and desires.

Many of us spend years trying to overcome our fears and find the strength to step into the unknown. We stay in uncomfortable situations that we have long outgrown. Deep within, we really desire evolution and expansion.

Clearly deciding what you want creates movement to conquer your restrictions and magnetize your desired outcomes. You will always be provided for when you follow your true path.

You must be willing to take the steps to cross the threshold. By overcoming barriers that we have previously made it sets in motion the initiation of change. Even small breakthroughs give a sense of power that motivates you to pursue your passion.

After taking the leap into our fears, we always want to go back to what is familiar. Knowing this fact gives you wisdom to recognize the pattern. When you have crossed a boundary, there is a fear of the unknown. Previously, there was a predictable outcome but now there is new territory to discover. Do not allow yourself to sabotage your achievements. Many people give up too soon.

Connect to your original excitement and feelings of accomplishment when you decided to make a change. That part of you wants to pursue your purpose. Know that you are never ready to cross the threshold when you do. The energy that is often thought of as fear is really excitement for the new.

Trust that you must be courageous enough to accomplish anything worthwhile. Taking a step toward your desires sets the process in motion. We are always supported by unseen forces when we trust and take a leap of faith.

Staying safe depletes our life energy. Our desire to return to old patterns is only so that we can predict the outcome. Remember that the predictable outcome is what you sought to break away from.

You can never go back to the familiar patterns peacefully once you have experienced the euphoria of pursuing your desires. This is because the shift has already occurred in your energy field and has been set in motion. It is time to celebrate and embrace the change.

He was intelligent and capable of any career path. He got the highest scores on all of his admittance exams. Logically, he should have pursued a difficult course of action that would guarantee him a significant income.

He went to college and settled into the routine of a mundane requirement of classes. He was the best student in every class, receiving the highest scores. He was the ideal student on the perfect path in his career world.

In high school he had pursued his passion of acting, singing and discovering his musical abilities. He loved the experience and felt he could passionately express his truest gifts. However, when it came the time to attend college, his logic persuaded him to choose the career that would provide the best financial stability.

He was miserable in his studies. He went through the motions of school but his heart yearned for the expression of his gifts in music. He continually told himself he could suppress his feelings and follow the path that everyone thought he should.

He became more depressed and shut down. The battle within him grew between following his heart's desire and doing what society encouraged by pursuing a prestigious career. There was nothing he was passionate or excited about anymore.

He finally decided to look into other opportunities. Still unwilling to let go of his distinguished career path, he gave himself permission to explore what made him happy. In his discovery he knew he could not live a life that did not allow him to do what made him thrive.

He gave up his scholarships and school and pursued an unconventional arena that helped him reunite with his true love, music. Listening to his heart, he discovered that he could live his passion and receive the income that he desired as well. He discovered that when he is doing his life's work all he needed would come to him.

Our inner knowing tells us when it is time to change course from the path we are on. Pursuing what comes naturally and trusting the flow is where you find your passion. The ease in change occurs when you let go of situations, beliefs or people that are no longer working for you. You internal system knows what is for your greatest good.

Our growth and aliveness come from allowing new ideas to form. Focus on what you want and it will come to you. Trust that letting go of one thing allows space for something better to come.

Exercise 9:

1. What situations are you still in that you know you have outgrown?

2. If you could have what you really want, how would it be different?

3. What is an area that you were most passionate about but you gave up on because of your fear to take the next step?

4. What step can you take to begin to pursue that passion again?

5. What is the true meaning of success to you?

6. What does success feel like? How does it look, sound, smell, taste... and even feel touch? Explore each aspect of success with your senses.

7. How can you use your success to contribute to the betterment of our world? What would be an expression of you that uniquely adds your energy to society?

Embrace Our True Essence

We all have innate spiritual powers that are the source of our healing. Healing encompasses much more than health problems and crises. It is the power that leads us to embrace our true essence.

Healing connects us to an effortless life path that brings us the most joy and satisfaction. The stability and strength from delving into the depths of our darkness awakens the discovery of how powerful we really are.

Higher states of awareness are available as we fully embrace our stillness. Our emptiness holds the possibility of freedom; for it is the space of receptivity. What we focus on is drawn to us and our emotions intensify that power.

Emptiness gives us a sense of freedom from attachment. The gifts of perceiving the world differently come by releasing our distorted views. It opens our receptivity for any possible outcome we desire.

We have the power to live a life that brings us the fullest joy and satisfaction. New perspectives in life open our gifts and allow the natural rhythms to flow. Healing bridges the gap and awakens our power to embrace freedom and movement.

We can create wholeness when we love, honor and fully express ourselves. All parts of us must participate to be in sync with this natural rhythm.

Healing is never complete. Healing occurs in a cyclic spiral rhythm that allows us to revisit patterns. As we pass through life experiences, we gain new awareness of our talents and wisdom.

Remaining firmly grounded in the earth, we receive nurturing life force energy that allows us to grow and expand in strength and power. We must honor our yearning for our connection to life that comes from self-discovery.

Listening to our inner direction allows us to consistently unite with the creative forces. We can experience the world differently. This state creates a life full of simplicity, peace and joy.

We can no longer ignore the voice of our desires. We must acknowledge our uniqueness and be the expression of who we are. We each have individual gifts to contribute to society as a whole.

Neuro Energetic Kinesiology

Elaine Lemon, an Advanced Practitioner and instructor of Neuro Energetic Kinesiology, specializes in distance healing, as well as Spiritual & Wellness coaching.

Kinesiology is a system that monitors stress imbalances through muscle testing. Neuro Energetic Kinesiology is a specialized Kinesiology that relates to detecting and correcting various imbalances that are due to the body's reaction to stress. The work is done holographically, which allows the practitioner to heal the specific aspect that relates to the whole.

Stress in the body can occur through emotional trauma and suppression, nutritional imbalances, injuries, lack of brain integration, nervous system dysfunctions and imbalances in meridian and chakra system, as well as other sources.

Kinesiology allows the body to give feedback about the subtle energy of the meridians. Meridians nourish the organs and their ability to function. Fundamental to our health and well being is balanced meridian energy.

Meridians are an intricate part of the interfacing circuits of the nervous system which connect to a complex network that affects the functioning of the whole body. When one of the meridians and its related circuits is switched off, it upsets the regularity and operation of the body.

Neuro Energetic Kinesiology effectively finds the sources and corrects the circuits that detrimentally affect one's ability to respond to stress and learning. Stress in the body is a compensation response from life experiences that influences our ability to function.

Compensation to stress may manifest in many areas of the body through the neurology, muscle, organs, glands, hormones, blood, and lymph. The stress imbalance can also be held in the spiritual centers of our system as well, which include our chakras, light bodies, aura, nadis and other systems.

The majority of the symptoms we have come from suppressing an issue or trauma, thus creating separation from the whole. Neuro Energetic Kinesiology uses muscle monitoring to access the stress and symptoms and rectify the pathway of the stress.

Balancing techniques allow the body to make corrections for optimal well-being. We as humans are a complex web or matrix that connects as a whole. By accessing the part of the system that is creating physical or emotional dysfunction, one can heal.

Our bodies store stress in the intricate system of our cells that carry an electrical frequency, chemical reactions, as well as magnetic influences. Our body's cells react to the source of stress.

Physical trauma, emotional stress, chemical toxicity exposure to pathogens, viruses, toxic metals, mycotoxins, chemicals, ionizing radiation, genetically modified foods, pesticides, weed killers, synthetic fertilizers, artificial sweeteners, drugs and geopathic and electrical stress cause the body to react through over compensation .

The body has cellular memory that creates a reaction by storing the information in our cells, muscle cells, cellular structures and neurons. When the DNA sequence is altered it creates a variation. The variation inhibits an enzyme and its coenzyme, which causes either shutting down of an essential biological process or an over-reactive immune response. The frequency and memory in the cellular structure blocks the pathway to create significant positive life changes.

The reactions and effects of stress are dependent on the intensity, location, and the perspective of an individual. Our bodies are designed to heal. Blockages of the body system pathways stop the alignment of well being.

Neuro Energetic Kinesiology corrects the imbalance in the pathway that restores the system to its original blueprint. The practitioner finds the stress and directs the body to release, integrate and align the system, giving the body the support it needs to create greater health and well-being.

Neuro Energetic Kinesiology is not a medical replacement. One should always seek a medical professional for diagnosis and treatment. Neuro Energetic Kinesiology is a specialized form of Kinesiology that supports other health technologies.

NeuroEnergetic Kineisology (NEK) is a specialized form of Energy Kinesiology which focuses on bridging the gaps of:

*Brain neurology and integration

*Incorporating cellular and human physiology

*Balancing hormones and neurotransmitters function

*Learning and memory balancing

*Unique formatting for chakras, light bodies, aura and spiritual centers

*Emotional pathways of the brain and emotional processing

Elaine Lemon

Elaine Lemon is the founder of Empower Wholeness LLC, an Advanced Certified Practitioner of Neuro Energetic Kinesiology and the Energy Kinesiology Association. She is a spiritual, health and wellness coach, specializes in distance healing and is an Earth Transition Practitioner.

Elaine is a Certified 'Heal Your Life' workshop leader, instructor for the International College of Neuro Energetic Kinesiology, an instructor for the Canyon School of Massage and Healing Arts, and a facilitator for Karlfeldt Healing Retreats.

Elaine is the co-author of the book *'Beyond Beautiful'* and *'Methods of the Masters'* and an Executive Producer of the documentary *Take it With You*.

Elaine's expansive work incorporates breakthroughs in brain neuroscience, brain integration, DNA helix activation, nutrition, body energy pathways, sensory integration, emotional processing, motivational heart-mind empowerment, conscious evolution and creating a sacred space through Earth and environment healing.

Elaine lives in Boise, Idaho loving her time with the two of her five children that live there. Elaine's personal journey of healing inspires others to fulfill their soul purpose and to engage fully in their spontaneous joy; navigating through the experiences of life and claiming wisdom, love, and power from the blueprint within.

www.ElaineLemon.com
www.EmpowerWholeness.com

Dedication:

Dedicated to all I inspire in your awakening journey.

Acknowledgements:

With much love and gratitude to my children who have exemplified the true meaning of unconditional love and inspired me to seize the moment. Bryce Lemon, Alyssa Lemon, Derek Lemon, Connor Lemon, and McKell Lemon. I love you forever. I like you for always. Deep gratitude to Dr. Michael Karlfeldt who lit my candle when my light had gone out. Robert K. Banks who has given me courage, support and strength; the pure example of compassion. Debby Kennedy who has gone above and beyond the duty of friendship. Howdy Ho! David Benoit who taught me through example true charity. Darren Truchot who willingly gave me hope through his generosity. Cindy Truchot for your consideration. Kim and Kaye Cherry who graciously blessed my life. To all the many souls that have been my strength and have taught me how to not only give but also receive. I AM who I AM because of love.

Bibliography:

Carol, Lee. Kyron *The Twelve Layers of DNA (An Esoteric Study of the Mystery Within)*. Sedona, AZ: Platinum Publishing House, 2010. Print.

Epstein, D.C., Donald M. *The 12 Stages of Healing*. San Rafael, CA: Amber-Allen Publishing, 1994. Print.

Prakasha, Padma, and Anaiya A. Prakasha. *Womb Wisdom Awakening the Creative Forgotten Powers of the Feminine*. Rochester, VT: Destiny Books, 2011. N. pag. Print.

Renaud, Gilbert, and Marie G. Rheault. *Total Biology of the Living Creatures*. N.p.: n.p., 2008. Print.

Singh, Narayan. *Messages From the Body*. N.p.: n.p., 1997. Print.

Tobar, Hugo, International College of Neuor Energetic Kinesiology Workshops & Certification, www.icnek.com

Wayman, Ronald, American College of Neuro Energetic Kinesiology www.icnek.net

ENDORSEMENTS FOR BLANCA COBB

"When you're ready to live life on your own terms, read Blanca Cobb's story in *Methods of the Masters: Inspiring and Uplifting Stories for Taking Your Happiness and Effectiveness in Life to the Next Level!* Blanca's sitting-at-the-edge-of-your-seat story of survival and triumph is a remarkable guide for anyone who's been knocked down, in one way or another, who is ready to take back their power. Through sharing her heroic journey, Blanca tears away self-doubt and fear through 3 surprisingly easy steps and helps us change our "someday" to "today!" Don't you deserve to make today the day you recognize your own worth and potential? Act fast. Buy this book!"

- Janine Driver, *New York Times* Best Selling Author of
  You Say More Than You Think and NEW author of *You Can't Lie to Me!*

"Does one stay trapped in the darkness of the past or break free? Blanca Cobb shares her courageous battle to free herself of past traumas and fears to create a fulfilling and genuine life. Blanca's story is heartfelt, real, and inspirational. Although you feel her pain and suffering, her victory over her fears and victimhood is awakening. Blanca's profound struggle to find her voice and create a life she always wanted will move all readers. Take the next step in your own life by using Blanca's wisdom as a beginning for your journey! A must read!"

- Dennis L. McKnight, Ph.D.
  Director and Owner of the Center for Cognitive Behavioral Therapy
  Adjunct Professor at the University of North Carolina at Greensboro

Chapter 3

Courage Can Come From Darkness: Overcoming Fear to Create a Life You Love

"Let your past push you forward,
not hold you back. Free yourself."
- *Blanca Cobb*

    "Keep moving," I told myself as I ran through the woods behind our house. "Run faster and you'll get there sooner." As I was twisting my way through the maze of the trees with arms outstretched to catch any stray limbs, I realized how much I loved summer. The trees were in full bloom, making it easier to hide behind their leaves. Just as an umbrella can shield you from the rain, the leaves can hide you from the world. I'd seen eight summers now, yet only roamed the woods for the past three. I knew which trees blocked the hot rays of the sun best and which ones were the easiest to climb. I'd forgotten about the old oak tree with its tangled roots poking out of the ground until my foot caught and I heard a loud thud. After I pushed myself up and started spitting out dirt, I realized that the thud was the sound of my breath escaping my body when I slammed into the ground.

    My eyes stung, but I didn't know if it was from the sweat that had rolled down my forehead or from a mixture of dirt and tears. It didn't matter. I got back up and used the inside of my shirt to wipe them. I ran again because my mission was to climb my way to safety. When I found my skyward portal, I climbed as high as I could to get away from the pain and humiliation. I settled my butt on my favorite tree branch and promised myself that I wouldn't let him hurt me anymore. Before I could figure out how to stop him, I had to heal my body from the pain of falling and the welts on my back, butt and legs that would soon show. I pushed the branches together in front of me so that I felt like I was protected by an impenetrable shield. The slight breeze soothed the heat from the pain and the sun, but I had to keep shifting my butt on the branch because sitting too long in one spot made the hurt more painful.

I loved sitting in the trees swinging my legs back and forth. Sometimes, I let my shoes drop from my feet so I could count the seconds it took for them to hit the ground. I liked listening to the wind rustle the leaves, particularly on a windy day; the louder and stronger the winds howled, the quieter were the echoes of the chaos in my head. I noticed the way the leaves frantically swayed by the sheer force of the wind and my mind immediately connected the image to the thought of millions of tiny white flags surrendering to the enemy. Surrender. Something I vowed never to do. I watched the squirrels and birds play and rummage for food. I thought ants were funny little insects, marching single file, one right behind the other to an unknown destination and wished I could follow. I envied their freedom. Against my mom's warnings, I climbed higher or swung monkey-like from branch to branch. Most of all, I loved being by myself and away from my mom's husband, and the woods offered me temporary peace and relief from the humiliation of the name-calling, yelling and beatings.

That day up in the tree, I fell out of it. I must've been 15 or so feet in the air when I fell. I landed mostly on my butt and lost my breath for a few moments. Although I was shaking, my lips were quivering and my butt was aching, unbelievably, I didn't get hurt. I stumbled around, hunched forward rubbing my butt bone with both of my hands. I guess it's like my mom has always told me- I've got angels watching over me. Many times growing up it didn't feel like my angels were anywhere near me. I wondered if they hid too. While I regained my bearings from the fall, my skin got goose bumps as I sensed a dark presence. I thought I may have hit my head too, until I looked up and saw his eyes staring at me. That's when I realized that I'd fallen up the rabbit hole back into my hell of reality. Worst of all, my promise to protect myself was broken within a matter of minutes. And you know what else? It was the first of many broken promises.

Throughout my childhood and adolescence, a familiar version of this scene repeated itself. As I got older the people and situations changed, but the end result was the same. I was hurt, betrayed and humiliated. Since I believed in hope, I believed I'd find healthy and lasting friendships. My hope, however, diminished over time with repeated disappointments. Those whom I trusted betrayed my friendship, and those whom I cared about humiliated me by starting and spreading rumors. By the time I graduated high school, I had few friends. Looking back, I realize I didn't believe in myself. I didn't believe in my worth as a person. As a result, I was an easy target for ridicule and the subsequent humiliation. I was silenced whenever I voiced opposing ideas and opinions to those who didn't care to hear them. I quickly learned to be seen, but not heard. I decided that the best way to keep friends was by hiding my real self and being the one to acquiesce. If I didn't cause any waves, then there'd be no storms. If only I knew how that decision would impact my life.

Fast forward 13 years with a new baby girl and a husband, I found myself in uncharted waters. I never understood the strength and depth of a mother's love until I became one. Although I loved being pregnant, I had a complicated pregnancy with preterm labor. My body cooperated and I gave birth to our daughter about 1 1/2 weeks early. She was the epitome of health, beauty and perfection. After she was born, I knew my life had new meaning. I was no longer living for myself, but also for her. Just like a genie coming out of a bottle after one hundred years of slumber, my desire to voice my opinions and for my opinions to be respected awakened with a vengeance. I was on a mission to correct the wrongs of my childhood by making hers right. My determination was strong, but my lack of experience left my strategy and execution a bit weak.

All well-meaning female relatives, these being grandmothers, mothers, aunts, sisters, cousins including the in-law versions- are eager to share their successful childrearing "suggestions" to help the newbie moms in bathing, caring, feeding, napping, sleeping and socializing of the babies. Well, I'm all about sharing ideas on how to raise children. As I quickly learned, there's a lot of trial and error in being a mother. Moms can learn from each other's tried and true ways. I believe in the adage "It takes a village to raise a child." However, I don't believe in having the enemy set up a tent in my village. Let me clarify what I mean. If moms don't take female relatives' suggestions then they shouldn't make snide remarks such as "Well, it worked for me." or "Your sister's kids don't seem to have the same problems as yours." or "You turned out O.K." or "Relax, a hair pull now and then only builds character." or "Crying is good for their lungs." My point is newbie moms need validation and support, not backhanded comments which only serve to alienate them from the family. No one wins in these situations, and especially not the babies.

I had more than one tiff with family members along the way about their forceful opinions on child-raising and their interactions with my baby girl. When she was six months old, I let a female relative hold her at a family get-together. Well, my baby girl wouldn't settle; she was fussy and I decided I wanted to calm her. To my surprise, I was told that "she (my baby) would be fine and to go eat dinner with the rest of the family." Initially I was speechless, but then I was beyond pissed. I couldn't believe the nerve of this female relative who refused to give me my baby. As much as I'd like to say I had the upper hand and got my baby back, I cannot. I got upset, cried silently, and sat obediently at the dinner table all the while listening to my baby cry in the room at the other end of the house. Within 15 minutes, this female relative chose to give me back my baby. After this incident, I realized that I couldn't protect my baby and be an effective mother if I didn't speak up. Knowing I'm the best mom for my baby girl isn't enough; I have to send this message to others by not waffling on my decisions and letting others know that my decisions aren't negotiable. In another incident, a male relative told my baby girl turned toddler she had "thunder thighs." Although my toddler didn't understand the meaning of his words, I did. I was offended and didn't see how her body type defined her as a person. Sure, some of you might be thinking adults make teasing comments about babies and children that they don't mean. I agree with you as long as the comments don't offend. However, repeated messages about one's body type can lead to low self-esteem, an outside-in source of validation and eating disorders. I wanted my then toddler to love herself as she is and having adults make comments contrary to my philosophy didn't settle with me. Well, instead of handling the situation myself, I gave my husband the ammunition he needed to win the battle. I, however, lost the war as I didn't have the courage to speak up. I defaulted to acquiescence and let myself down. My confidence waxed and waned depending on my audience. With the tough, head strong personalities, I backed down.

Somewhere along the way as a newbie mom, I decided it was time to stop taking baby steps and jump into assertiveness and confidence in order to be the rock-star mom that my children (we've since had a son) deserved and expected. Many times I was uncomfortable and muddled through discussions with others. If you'd been a fly on the wall, you would've seen my face flush or turn red, fidgety hands, closed body language all the while speaking my truth. In time, my body language matched my words. Family relatives knew I meant what I said. Guess what? They backed off. Notice, I didn't say happily. Nonetheless, they accepted I was a mom not to be messed with. My mom characterizes me as "la madre leona" which means "the mother lion" in Spanish. Yes, I agree with her perception. I'm protective of my children and like most moms, I want only the best for them. Part of the giving them the best is living the best version of me.

Allowing my 'mommy voice' to be heard was empowering. I felt confident in my ability to speak up for my children and for myself as a mother. You know what? It feels good to speak up when something isn't quite right. To have my opinions accepted and respected is a great feeling. I felt like I mattered. Most importantly, I mattered to me. I couldn't believe all these years I'd shut my mouth and hid the true me for other people's agendas. At the time, acquiescence worked. It worked because I wanted to be an accepted and valued family member and friend. My strategy backfired because I was accepted, but not valued. I now realize it's hard to value someone who doesn't know her own worth. Well, I had enough and acquiescence wasn't an option anymore. I had to figure out a way to be true to myself in all aspects of my life. I felt something was missing. I felt unbalanced. I had to find ways to live authentically and to cleanse myself of the impurities I had allowed. For several months, I was mad at myself and my life. Anger is an overpowering entity and, at times, I felt I was losing touch with myself. I pursued discarded interests as a way to re-establish a lost connection with myself. I learned to shoot handguns at an indoor gun range and practiced martial arts for those just-in-case moments. These kick-butt activities allowed me to relieve pent up anger and stress. I felt more confident, powerful and connected to myself. Re-establishing a relationship with myself was easier than I thought. The tougher re-connection was with other people. After so many years of being passive, I wasn't quite sure how speak my mind and be heard.

While finding ways to live authentically, I created all kinds of 'smart-Aleck' remarks which I call zingers. I think my zinger creations were a way to silently yell at the world. A friend of mine who's just as edgy as I am loved my zingers. I bounced all kinds of zinger sayings off of her. We laughed, talked and shared stories about how the zingers resonated with each of us. At some point, I thought about putting the zingers on T-shirts for women so others could wear their own confidence.

With my husband's support, my concept for a T-shirt line for sexy, savvy and suggestive women was born. I named my T-shirt company, SPRiSH®, a word I created which combines my "Spanish" heritage with that of my friend's (the one I just told you about) "Irish" heritage. Here's the thing about my T-shirt line: SPRiSH® is for confident women who march to the beat of their own drummers. SPRiSH® identifies with women who are comfortable with themselves and who aren't easily influenced by others' opinions.

My T-shirt designs are fun, flirty, edgy, and make a statement for you. What woman doesn't want to be noticed? What man doesn't want to be with a confident woman who unleashes her moxie?

The development of SPRiSH® moved forward at full speed. I collaborated with my graphic designer, who takes the abstract concepts in my mind and together, we artistically express my zingers into designs. I consulted with my intellectual property attorney about trademark and copyright rights for my company name and T-shirt designs. I worked with a screen printer who transfers my artistically detailed zingers onto finished products. I developed an e-commerce store with a website developer to sell my super cool and fun T-shirts online. The T-shirt line was coming along, and I embraced and lived my true self. Sure, my confidence waxed and waned at various times. At first, I didn't want anyone to know I was the woman behind my brand, SPRiSH®. I wanted to sell my T-shirts anonymously. I wanted to continue to hide from myself and others. I had hidden from my past and my life for so long that invisibility was comfortable. As much I believed in my company and my platform of confident women, I was scared to expose myself to ridicule and criticism. I worried about what others would think and say about me and my T-shirt designs. Remember earlier when I said that I didn't make waves so a storm wouldn't follow? Well, this was another time I wanted to be passive.

As life would have it, I met two extraordinary people who, unbeknownst to them (until they read this story), helped me finally let go of my past and embrace my future. A couple of years ago while I was browsing the internet, I saw a *Today Show* clip on Janine Driver, President of the Body Language Institute (BLI) in Washington D.C., who was promoting her *New York Times* Best Selling body language book, *You Say More Than You Think*. I didn't realize I could use body language to succeed in life. I imagined the peace and confidence I'd have if I could use these techniques to figure out people's intent during both personal and professional interactions. The image was so powerful that I signed up to learn more. Janine is an incredibly confident and powerful woman who is intelligent, funny and charismatic. She has an uncanny ability to uncover the strengths in others they don't realize they have. She encouraged me to step out of my comfort zone in my class presentations of the body language material. By the end of the course, Janine told me I was a natural with refined instincts and she saw a lot of potential in me. She asked me to join her as an instructor at the Body Language Institute. I was a mixed bag of emotions; from excitement to disbelief to doubt. Nonetheless, I relished the possibility of becoming my own powerhouse knowing I couldn't be as easily fooled anymore.

In her course "Brand Yourself and Get on TV" that Janine co-teaches with Terence Noonan (a five time EMMY® award winning producer who's the executive producer of *Anderson Live*, Anderson Cooper's daytime talk show), I learned ways to brand and pitch SPRiSH®, my T-shirt company. Terence is a powerhouse in his own right. He's witty, hilarious and knows how to bring the best out of people. In one of the class exercises, I had to pitch SPRiSH® to Terence. Within a minute of my pitch, he stopped me and said something like, "Blanca, you have a great T-shirt concept. How can I as a customer believe in your product if you can't even tell me what's so great about your T-shirt line?" And then he asked me the million dollar question: "What are you afraid of?" That's a question I've mulled over thousands of times like a cow ruminates on feed.

METHODS OF THE MASTERS

One morning several months later, the answer struck me as hot water splashed my skin while I showered. Past memories flooded my mind as I saw visions of being pinned to the ground, my blood seeping into the carpet, high school yearbooks scribbled with "I hate Blanca," hard stares and turned backs, and the intense loneliness I suffered in silence. With arms wrapped tight across my middle, I quivered from the realization that I was afraid of myself. I've broken so many promises to protect myself from harm, hurt, betrayal and deceit that I didn't trust myself anymore. That's when I made the connection to Terence's question. I was afraid I wouldn't be able to protect myself from the risk, criticism, success and/or failure of SPRiSH®. I was afraid of both success and failure, and all that the two encompass. That's partly the reason why I wanted to be the anonymous owner of SPRiSH®. I didn't believe I could take care of and protect myself. Subconsciously, I was sabotaging my future by giving other people's opinions of me more credence than my opinions of myself.

My life was about to change course yet again, reaching higher on my skyward portal; only this time there was no tree. Just me, making it happen. I have to take you back a little bit in my story in order to move forward. Remember I told you Janine asked me to be an instructor at the Body Language Institute? Before I could make this happen, I wanted extensive training. A few months after her "Branding Yourself and Get on TV" class, Janine handpicked 13 people to be a part of her Detecting Deception Power Team and receive her exclusive training on how to bust the liars in your life which was part of her second book, *You Can't Lie to Me*. I was one of 13 selected for this intense training. We learned her systematic approach to determining if and when there is more to someone's story. We reviewed reels and reels of footage of known liars and convicted felons searching for both verbal and nonverbal "tells" of deception. We tested our skills on each other to figure out who was lying. At one point, we weren't doing so well in following her method, so Janine upped the ante and offered the best and most improved interrogator a free cruise on her BLI at Sea course. Guess what? I won! In fact, Janine asked me to teach a course on analyzing verbal statements for both verbal and nonverbal tells of deception on the cruise. I'm proud to say I rocked my presentation and I received a standing ovation.

Not only did I train with Janine, I trained with other recognized interrogation, interview and detecting deception experts who train law enforcement at both the national and local levels. I made my first splash in the national and local media with the trial of former U.S. Senator and Presidential candidate, John Edwards. Since I had been traveling to training courses and to the Body Language Institute, I didn't attend as much of the trial as I wanted. The first day I attended the trial, the courthouse was packed mostly with reporters and some curious court spectators. I sat beside two women in the overflow room. Before court was called into session, I turned to them and introduced myself. During conversation, I learned that Sheeka Strickland and Nicole Ferguson were reporters on assignment covering the trial for FOX 8 WGHP News in High Point. When they asked my connection to the trial, I explained I was a detecting deception and body language expert. They were intrigued and curious about my profession. I shared personal stories of the ways I used my skills to identify a juror in a different trial who wasn't forthcoming about his personal involvement and/or that of a family member in a violent crime. As it turned out, the District Attorney for the case discovered the juror had lied, and he was dismissed from jury duty during the trial. I also shared the story of another time that I caught a judge minimize his statement in a casual conversation with me. During the course of the trial, Sheeka Strickland contacted me asking for an interview about John Edwards' body language walking to and from the Federal courthouse. This first interview with Sheeka led to other media interviews with Good Morning America, CNN, FOX, CBS, ABC, NBC affiliates among others. I've been interviewed about John Edwards' body language, the nonverbal signs of child sexual predators like Jerry Sandusky and about the Colorado theater shooting suspect.

What started out as a personal endeavor to learn how to detect deception turned into another business opportunity. I started, own and run TruthBlazer, where I offer trial consulting, keynote presentations and detecting deception courses. I also travel to Washington D.C. frequently, as I'm now a Senior Instructor at the Body Language Institute where I share my people-reading skills and techniques on how to analyze hot spots in both verbal and written statements. As an entrepreneur, I'm insanely busy and sometimes think I've gotten in over my head as I learn to run two businesses and juggle my time among family, work and myself. However, I am passionate about both of my companies, SPRiSH® and TruthBlazer, and I know that I made the right choice to launch them both.

I'm having a lot of fun reaching my potential and seeing just how high my star will get. I know I'll face other obstacles in my life. I'll have to find ways to move around or eliminate those obstacles. I'm no longer the little girl who hid from herself and her life in order to survive. I'm now a woman who embraces her strengths, courage, wisdom, confidence, commitment, determination, creativity, perseverance, imperfections and limitations. Right now, I'm enjoying my journey, and I'm open to all kinds of possibilities. Although I don't know what will happen in my future, I know I'll be O.K. because I believe in me!

I'm glad you stopped by and read part of my story. I've got many other stories, but that's for another time. Now that you know a little about me, let's talk a little about you. Do you believe in you? I was surprised to learn that millions of people who suffer from fear have had difficulties standing up to life. For almost ever, I thought I was the only one who hid in trees in a false illusion of protection. In a weird kind of way, it's reassuring to know I wasn't the only one who struggled with fear. Knowing that others struggled normalized my experiences so that they didn't seem insurmountable. I've heard somewhere that there's strength in numbers. Every now and again, I imagine how different my life would've been if I had realized sooner that I didn't trust myself to protect me. Well, all the speculating won't change my past. After searching for years, I finally found the right path that is leading me to a fulfilling life. Do you ever wonder how you can manage your fears to create a life you love? Good, I'm happy to know you do. Now, let me share three tips I learned along my journey to help you conquer your fears.

1. **Purge Yourself:** No, I'm not talking about your lunch or your closet. I'm talking about purging the areas of your life where you are holding yourself back. To do so, you have to critically examine the ways in which you've failed yourself. Reflect on any and all past relationships, careers, education, and experiences. Other areas to consider are: intimacy, being alone, success, finances, failure, victimization, re-victimization, career, promotions, future, parenting, divorce, health, death, acceptance and rejection, and feelings of inadequacy. Anytime you find yourself saying "I wish I had done..." or "What if..." or "If I could redo..." you'll find the answers. You won't be able to manage your fears until you

know what you're afraid of.

A victim mentality, helplessness and not feeling in control contribute to feelings of fear. Now that you've identified what's holding you back, spend time figuring out how you're perpetuating the victim role. Do you find yourself: blaming others, including your parents, for your failures, saying to yourself that you're not good enough or you'll never "get it," wishing you had a better childhood, never putting yourself first, criticizing yourself for perceived shortcomings, telling yourself no one has ever believed you or in you, believing your powerless and helpless, highlighting your failures? If you answered "yes" to any of these questions then you, my friend, having been playing a victim role in your life. These destructive thoughts not only keep you in the victim role, but also perpetuate your feelings of fear.

How do you break free from the victim role? Begin by accepting responsibility for keeping yourself in the victim role. I'm talking about the "poor me" messages that you communicate to yourself and others about having been a victim. Most people in the victim role don't understand how their thoughts about their victimization impact their interactions with themselves and other people. They don't realize if they change their perceptions of having been a victim, then they can change the course or outcomes of their lives. Let me give you an example of what I mean. Let's say you were bullied as a teen. Your peers incessantly ridiculed you, called you derogatory names, spread rumors about you, and sometimes, they physically attacked you. Once an outgoing teen, you withdrew from life, the bullies, as well as your family and friends. You lost interest in the activities you once enjoyed. You stopped studying and your grades fell for a period of time. Not sure how you even got accepted in the first place, you get yourself together and graduate from college. Now faced with having to start a life as an independent adult, you move to a different city where you land a job and find a romantic partner. All goes well until it's not. You figure out a co-worker is claiming credit for your project ideas and you're bubbling hot. The nerve of your co-worker to pass along your ideas as her own. You decide to set the record straight by speaking up. You talk to your co-worker who manages to maximize her contributions to the project while minimizing yours. She claims that the project is a joint effort and everyone gets credit, not just you. In fact, she claims that you took her project ideas. At the end of the discussion, you don't feel heard or validated. You feel sorry for yourself and chalk up the experience as yet another disappointment. Subconsciously, you decide that you're not good enough just like in high school when you were bullied. You think there's something wrong with you for people to continue to disregard you and your feelings. Instead of thinking of different ways to be heard, you accept your co-worker's views of the situation as fact and final. You just give up. Whoa! Slow down. Back up. Good people suffer bad things every day. I don't understand why it happens so I can't begin to explain it. I just know that we have to reframe our experiences to live healthy and effective lives.

Continuing to sabotage yourself with a victim mentality only serves to emotionally stifle you with fear and self-doubt. I believe that you have to be a problem-solver and figure out what you can change in current and future situations. In this example, check your notes and emails for who was responsible for what in the project. If you can't change this particular situation, then plan for the next collaborative project with this co-worker. Set in place ways to document everyone's responsibility so there's no misrepresentation at the end. Better yet, figure out her strengths and pre-assign her certain tasks where she'll excel and not need to sabotage your contributions. Spend some time looking at the situation from her point of view. What does she have at stake that she feels the need to take credit for ideas that aren't hers? Perhaps, you re-structure the group dynamics for the next project. Invite another co-worker to join in as buffer as well as a contributor. Think outside the box. The solutions are endless. My point is to take active control of your situation by problem solving. Effective problem solving will increase your self confidence and personal effectiveness. Remember, you are responsible for creating a life you love.

2. Challenge Yourself: Think of an interest you have that pushes you out of your comfort zone. Have you ever wanted to shoot skeet, learn self defense, figure out the CIA secrets to uncover deception, analyze handwriting or body language, learn negotiating skills, fight with samurai swords, pole dance, parasail over the ocean, perfect your poker skills, or participate in a performance driving school? Think of any activity that pushes your limits. Why? A lot of times fears are based on faulty thinking and exaggerations of the facts. We tell ourselves "no" because we don't like something, we don't know how to do something, or we're not good at something. Yet we haven't even tried the blooming activity! We shortchange ourselves of the variety in life by always sticking with the familiar. On a side note, the variety over familiarity concept is one of my SPRiSH® T-shirt designs. One of the best gifts you can give yourself for stretching your comfort zone is the realization you are stronger and more powerful than what you think! Show off your bad-ass-ness (Is this even a word?) What you are waiting for? Act now to discover what you are made of!

3. Believe in Yourself: We strive to surround ourselves with people who accept us for who we are, imperfections and all. Wait. What did I just say? The statement deserves to be repeated. We seek out people who accept us for who we are, including our imperfections. How can we expect others to accept and value us if we don't believe in ourselves and accept our own imperfections and limitations? Validation should come from within us, as we know ourselves best. We understand who we are, what we're made of, and why we are unique. Yet so many times we look for validation from others and the validation goes hand-in-hand with the length of the relationship. When the relationship ends we lose sight of our own importance because the link between our significance and the relationship is broken. With the relationship gone, we become afraid because the outside validation of who we are doesn't exist anymore. We get lost. Pure and untainted confidence comes from within us, not from other people. At the end of the day, we answer to ourselves. I learned along my journey of healing that it's none of my business what other people think of me even though I'm quite curious at times. What matters is what I think of myself.

Let's apply my 'believe in yourself' philosophy to the incredible story of Sylvester Stallone, an American actor, director and screenwriter. In his late 20's, Stallone struggled to make a living. As much as he tried to land a movie role, it didn't happen. Movie agents told him he was ugly with his droopy eyes, sounded funny with his slurred speech and didn't belong in front of a camera. Stallone's unique look and voice resulted from a forceps injury that occurred at birth which caused a partial facial paralysis. Tensions were high at home with his then wife because there wasn't any money to pay bills or buy food. At the height of his desperation, he sold his beloved dog, Butkus, for a negotiated price of $25.00

in front of a local liquor store. Despite the loss, he persevered. After watching a boxing match between Muhammad Ali and Chuck Wepner, Stallone got the inspiration to write "Rocky," a screenplay about an unknown boxer who fights the match of his life to prove he's got what it takes to go the distance, within three days. Stallone, ever persistent and determined, pitched the screenplay to anyone who would listen. Repeatedly he was told the plot was predictable, overplayed and stupid.

As luck would have it, Stallone met two movie producers, Robert Chartoff and Irwin Winkler, at a casting call- which by the way, he didn't land. On his way out of the door, Stallone casually mentioned he was a writer and asked the producers if they would read his screenplay. Intrigued, they accepted his invitation. The producing duo loved the screenplay and offered 100 thousand dollars, which was more money than Stallone ever thought possible. Before making their offer, Chartoff and Winkler didn't realize a non-negotiable contract stipulation was that Stallone would star as the lead. No deal. The producing duo didn't want to risk the film on an unknown actor when Ryan O'Neal, Burt Reynolds or Robert Redford could catapult the film. Even with hunger pangs for money, Stallone declined the offer. Incredulous! How could Stallone walk away from such a massive amount of money? The answer is simple. Stallone believed in himself. Rocky's life struggles in the screenplay paralleled Stallone's struggles in his real life. Stallone decided no other man could portray the emotional depth and complexities of Rocky better than himself. Chartoff and Winkler contacted Stallone again within a couple of weeks and offered him 250 thousand dollars for the screenplay with Stallone out of his own movie. No deal. Stallone walked away from the offer. As Stallone tells the story (and no, not to me), at its highest the offer was 360 thousand dollars. Yet again, Stallone walked away from the deal because he wouldn't be cast in the title role. Finally, the two producers offered Stallone 35 thousand dollars along with the lead role. As much as Chartoff and Winkler believed in the potential of the movie, they thought it might tank with Stallone as the lead and wanted to minimize their financial risk. With a budget of just under one million dollars and a production time of less than one month, the "Rocky" movie grossed over 200 million dollars and won an Oscar® for best picture. Wow! Stallone's unrelentingly belief in himself paid off. He believed in his worth as a man and as an actor.

What happened to Butkus? I'm glad you asked. About one and one-half months after Stallone sold Butkus for $25.00, he stalked the liquor store in the hopes Butkus's new owner was a frequent shopper. On the third day of his stake out, Stallone saw Butkus's new owner and negotiated to buy Butkus back, to no avail. The new owner said he loved the dog and no amount of money would entice him to sell. To the tune of 15 thousand dollars and a part in the "Rocky" movie, Stallone walked away with his companion. When you watch the film again, you'll see Butkus in his original role right beside Stallone.

My wish for you is that you quell your fears and find peace. Applying the message learned from "Rocky," I leave you with this parting thought that I've adapted from Stallone: "Everyone has some fight and a lot of 'Rocky' in them." Now, go out there champ, and conquer the life you've always wanted!

Live Your Possibilities!

BLANCA COBB

Blanca Cobb is a mompreneur of two businesses, SPRiSH® and TruthBlazer, turned writer. She blogs about women and confidence as well as body language and detecting deception secrets as they relate to children, adolescents, parenting, romance, business and everyday life. In her writings, Blanca draws on her personal experiences, cutting-edge psychological and deception research and her background in psychology from the University of North Carolina at Chapel Hill and North Carolina State University. Blanca loves great stories, hearty laughs and adventurous friends. Blanca, her husband and their children live in North Carolina where she is currently working on her next book.

Blanca would love to hear from you. You can drop her a line at blanca@truthblazer.com. Follow her on Facebook at facebook.com/blancacobb and Twitter @BlancaCobb.

www.truthblazer.com
www.sprish.com

Chapter 4

It's All About Relationships

Introduction:

Relationships. They are the threads that form the very fabric of our lives. And whether we like it or not, the evidence seems clear: The quality of our lives depends upon the quality of our relationships. I don't know about you, but I wasn't taught a whole lot about consciously creating healthy, positive relationships. In fact, most of what I learned about relationships was how to manipulate, dominate and control people. And when I wasn't doing that, I was busy building a wall around me so that no one could love me or get too close.. and if no one could love me or get too close, no one could hurt me, and I was safe. If any of this sounds familiar to you, welcome to the Club. Most people are terrified of intimacy. But that's not the worst part. The worst part is t more than anything, most people want the very thing that terrifies them -- the ability to give and receive love freely.

The good news is that with a few simple skills and the willingness to be vulnerable, you can create healthy, positive, vibrant relationships starting now. The techniques and ideas presented in this chapter are specifically designed for you, and they are "all about relationships."

So if you want to learn about how to deal with people who push you away, it's here. If you want to learn how to handle it when someone betrays you, it's here. And if you want to learn a thing or two about dealing with people who drive you nuts, it's here. If you decide to continue reading, that's great. But just remember -- no one ever learned how to swim by reading about water. At some point, they had to jump in. By all means, read. And then ACT. Make a call, schedule a meeting and put these ideas into action. By doing so, you will have become the solution you seek. But the best part is, you will have created a context for your life that will easily sustain the very thing you've always wanted... to love and be loved.

"Everyone thinks about changing the world,
but no one thinks of changing themselves." - Leo Tolstoy

Three Surprising Lessons You Can Learn From a Frog

The Teacher Appeared

A trickle of red blood oozed out of its back. My heart sank. "You poor thing," I whispered, as I bent down to take a closer look at the fat, green frog sitting in my driveway, nearly invisible among a pile of orange, green and brown leaves. "I'm not gonna hurt you," I said, and tried to nudge the frog onto the grass with the edge of my boot, but it just sat there. The more I tried to move it, the more it bled. I started to cry. "I am so, so sorry," I thought. Little did I know this was the first of many lessons the frog had in store for me that morning.

The Student Is Ready

My mind raced to figure out how this could have happened. Did I run over it? No, I couldn't have. I had just pulled into the driveway and stepped out of the car, and there it was. If I had run over it, it would never have survived. Did I step on it? Impossible! How could I step on a frog on and not know it? What should I do? Should I put it out of its misery? Should I scoop it up and move it onto the grass? How could I have done this? In the end, I left the bleeding frog alone in the middle of the driveway and walked away. Feeling helpless and guilty, I said a quick prayer, hoping the frog would heal itself and hop to freedom. Chalk up Lesson #2 from Mr. Frog to me.

Yet Another Epiphany on the Treadmill

Out of nowhere, it hit me. "That little s--t," I said out loud just as I finished my last sprint. "Outsmarted by a frog!" Just to be sure, I ran outside to check the exact spot where the purported bleeding, dying frog was left to fend for itself. Sure enough, it was gone. "Good for you, little buddy," I shouted, hoping he could receive my heartfelt admiration for his cleverness. The third and final lesson was now complete, delivered by one of the most unusual teachers of my lifetime.

Lesson #1: If You Think Something is Bleeding and Dying, You Tend To Leave It Alone

Mr. Frog, it seems, was never bleeding at all. (But you already knew this, didn't you? :) Years of evolution caused the frog to ooze "red stuff" out of its back whenever it felt threatened. I guess the edge of my boot trying to nudge him into the grass qualified. Being the genius that he was, he knew that if I thought he was bleeding and dying, I'd leave him alone and eat something else. And guess what? I did.

Lesson #2: Some People Are Just Like Frogs

Have you ever been in a relationship with someone who makes it nearly impossible to get close to them? You try to touch them, to get close to them, and- like the frog- they begin to bleed (metaphorically speaking.) Often times, they'll do something that makes you move away- and move away fast. Maybe they lie to you. Maybe just when you start to feel connected, they pick a fight over absolutely nothing. Or maybe they begin finding fault with you where no fault exists, just to make themselves feel safe. All I know is that there are some people who, no matter what you do, won't let you touch them. The closer you get, the more they bleed. The more they bleed, the more you try to get close to them; the more you try, the more they sabotage your efforts. Eventually, you get the message. GO AWAY. And, sure enough, you do. You go away.

Lesssson#3: Just Because Something Bleeds When You Touch It, Doesn't Mean It Has Anything To Do With You

Like frog, like human. Self protection, it seems, comes in many forms. People do lots of weird things to push love away so that they can feel safe. Why do people do it? Lots of reasons. To be sure, somewhere along the way they learned that love = pain. After having met and been illuminated by Mr. Frog, I now know that when I encounter these seemingly bizarre behaviors in others, that they have nothing to do with me. They never have. And they never will.

Whatever evolutionary impulse that causes frogs to bleed when we try to touch them, it was installed long before we showed up. The best we can do in human relationships is to know that there is an inherent need within each and every one of us to feel safe. Some of us meet this safety need in healthy ways through heart-to-heart talks mixed with honesty, the courage to be vulnerable, a good dose of self esteem and the willingness to be seen by one another. We consciously choose to use the tools of our humanity to allow and even invite others to touch us, to love us, even though we're scared to death. We decide not to bleed because we know that we are not frogs, and that love -- real love -- is nothing to be afraid of.

Other people, no matter what you do, simply bleed.

Knowing this, the next time I encounter a human who acts like a frog when I get too close, I'll know just what to do. I won't apologize or take it personally. I won't try to turn myself inside out to convince them that I am the savior who will heal all of their past hurts and make it all go away. I won't chase them into the grass, put them in a container and try to change them from a frog into a prince.

Instead, I'll say a quick prayer, take a step back, nod, smile, love them anyway... and I'll keep walking.

How To Get Back Up When Someone You Love Knocks You Down

You suspected something was going on. Now, you don't think- you know that someone you love and trust has betrayed you. What do you do next? Open your mind and heart for three uncommon psycho-spiritual strategies that will help you heal, breathe and yes, love again.

Woman Meets Perfect Man

From the moment they met, she knew he was "the one". There was just something about him, she'd tell me. Physically, he was perfect. Just her type – jet black hair, green eyes, killer smile, and the body of Adonis. She dubbed him, "The King of Text Messages," and he swept her off her feet. No sooner would she wake up and roll over to check her phone, than there would be a message waiting for her: "Hey beautiful, just thinkin' about you." The fact that he made her laugh until she couldn't breathe and loved watching old Cary Grant movies till 2 am was just the beginning.

And yes, they spent days in bed. And yes, he did "that" better than any man in the history of the Universe. And yes, they traveled, got stoned, played cards, talked all night and intertwined toes under the covers on Sunday mornings. She loved him, and more than anything, she dreamed of a life with him that included a white picket fence and a lock box for all of their porn. He was, for her, the perfect man.

Until he wasn't.

Woman Meets Imperfect Man

When I picked up the phone, I could barely understand her she was crying so hard. As I listened to her retell the story, I felt like I was listening to a writhing animal moaning in the middle of the road who was just hit by a car. She wasn't just crying into the phone. She was wailing. "Piece of s—t, mother f--ker! How could he do this to me?" she screamed. "How does someone you love look you straight in the eye and lie to you?" Her sobs were uncontrollable. "My God, my God," she bawled. "How could he have done this Cheri? How does the man you love sleep with your best friend?"

It's a good question.

How does anyone betray someone they love? The answers are many and complex, but one thing's for sure: If this or something close to this hasn't happened to you yet, it will. This isn't meant to sound pessimistic, but it's highly unlikely that you will pass through this lifetime without at least one painful, heart-wrenching moment like the one described above. The details of the story aren't really the point. Betrayal happens between lovers, business partners and friends every day. All of us will inevitably wake up one day to find ourselves looking into the eyes of someone we loved and trusted and hear ourselves say, "How could you do this to me?" None of us who are alive are immune.

Betrayal's Choices

So now what? What's a normal human to do? There are lots of choices with this one. You could go on anti-depressants. You could smoke a whole lotta pot. You could get mad and stay married. You could pretend like it never happened. You could close the business, get your own lover or get your own lawyer and sue them for "everything they've got." You could ignore one of life's most powerful wake-up calls and find yourself years later, a little older, a little grayer, a little fatter, sitting in the same bar, on the same stool, telling the same life story you told last year over the same beer, not noticing that the people around you stopped listening and caring a long, long time ago.

Or you could do what most of us were never, ever taught to do.

You could wake up and get grateful.

Did I just say, grateful? Yes, I know. It sounds crazy, doesn't it? You're probably wondering: "Why in the world would anyone in their right mind want to become grateful when someone they love just ripped their heart out?"

For starters, being grateful doesn't mean you're not angry. It doesn't mean that whatever they've done doesn't hurt like hell. It doesn't mean you don't want to take a sledgehammer to their newly waxed car or even their head. It doesn't mean you forgive and forget. And it certainly doesn't mean that in order to be a good person, you choose to stay in the relationship.

It does mean that unlike most people, you choose to be grateful because you are simply unwilling to be a victim; you realize that when the tsunami of human relationships hits you, gratitude is a spiritual state of mind that opens the floodgates of life's lessons that would otherwise remain hidden; you choose gratitude because unlike most people, you recognize that <gasp> you co-created this event consciously or unconsciously, and that nothing happens in your life without your participation; finally, you choose gratitude because you want to use this painful situation to learn, to grow, to evolve, and to never, ever have to repeat this lesson again.</gasp>

Three Ways To Get Grateful

If you are ready, as Robert Frost wrote, "to take the road less traveled by," here are three ways you can choose to use gratitude to grow, evolve and bounce back even stronger when someone you love knocks you down:

1. See rightly Spiritual teacher Eric Butterworth writes that all spiritual growth is the result of "right seeing." Right seeing is the ability to see through a situation into the truth of it using spiritual eyes, rather than seeing it through the eyes of the world. The question becomes, what does it mean to see with spiritual eyes? It means to take the focus off of "what and why they did this to me" and put the focus where it belongs- on you. Now that your focus is where it belongs, you are positioned to ask the right questions.

2. Ask brutal questions I have a friend who was brutally raped repeatedly by four men for over 17 hours. Unthinkable, isn't it? When I asked her how she healed from this experience, she taught me a lesson I'll never forget. "I decided from the beginning that I was going to tell myself that they didn't do anything TO me," she said. "I decided to see it as something they did FOR me." (Excuse me. FOR YOU?) She went on to explain that she refused to be a victim; that she was going to use this experience to grow as a woman and as a spiritual warrior. Instead of asking herself, "Why did they DO this to me?", she chose to ask a brutally enlightening question: "What is this experience doing FOR me?" She then went on to write and publish a book as a result of the answers she received.

If you are ready to grow from your experience, a good place to start is to ask yourself brutal questions; questions like, "What role did I play in co-creating this situation? What didn't I want to see that I now see? What truth am I afraid to face? What is this situation teaching me about ME?" When my client Sharon asked this question after discovering her business partner was stealing from her, she discovered the truth that was trying to emerge from her: she was terrified that if she confronted him, she'd be alone… and she didn't believe she couldn't make it on her own.

What's your truth? Within the seeds of your betrayal are life-changing lessons waiting to emerge. But they can't emerge without your participation. You have to dig deep, muster all the courage you have, and ask seriously brutal questions. And by all means, have the Kleenex handy because the answers that come are often more painful than the betrayal itself.

3. Own Your S—T His name was John Bradford, and as he witnessed prisoners being led to their death as he rotted in the Tower of London, he uttered his now famous phrase, "There but for the grace of God go I." How humble and wise to turn away from judgment and condemnation of others and openly admit that on some level, "I, too, have done the same." This simple phrase is a profound recognition of the spiritual truth that we are all mirrors for one another. And if you are my mirror, whatever I think you have "done" to me, I've done to me, too. Just as you've lied to me, I've lied to me by pretending I didn't see what was happening in our relationship right in front of me. Just as you've stolen from me, I've stolen from me by living in fear and settling for less than what I deserve. Just as you've cheated on me, I've cheated on me by not telling you what I've been feeling and hiding from the truth about how I really feel. Just as you've abandoned me, I've abandoned me by not loving and honoring me the way I need to love and honor myself.

Admitting this is both painful and enlightening. When you feel hurt and victimized by someone's behavior and find yourself screaming, "I'd NEVER do that to you!", wait for the storm to pass. And when you can think and breathe and have stopped plotting their death, ruthlessly search your soul for the ways you've done the same thing to yourself. Or to someone else.

In a nutshell, own your s--t.

Within a very short period of time, you'll find that your judgment softens. It has to. Compassion and judgment are not happy bedfellows. By using the betrayal as a mirror into the hidden corners of your own life, you begin to see that you (shock of all shockers) are not so different from "them" after all.

The Conclusion Of Imperfect Man Meets Imperfect Woman

It's been a few years, but these two imperfect humans are now good friends. He is happily unmarried, living with his new lover in their cluttered cottage home on the lake. She is dating a divorced plastic surgeon who not only promises his fidelity, but who is also giving her a free breast augmentation this summer for her 40th birthday. Occasionally, if you can believe it, the four of them get together for laughs, steaks, dirty Martini's and carefully re-constructed stories of their past. It's weird, I know. But it works.

Betrayal, pain and disappointment in relationships are inevitable. But bitterness, stagnation and becoming a career victim are a choice. By choosing gratitude, you become that rare human who uses their free will to see with spiritual eyes, ask brutal questions and own their s--t. You become someone who doesn't just talk about making the world a better place, but lives it by being a walking, breathing example of someone who defines their very life by the progression of their growth. When you choose gratitude, you not only enrich your own life, but mine too. Who knows? Because of you, I just might wake up, stop telling my story and actually notice that the bar stool next to me is empty, and by God, there's no one there to listen.

And for that, all I can say is, I am eternally grateful.

Got Conflict? Why The Person Driving You Nuts Just May Be Your Greatest Teacher

The following excerpts are from actual conversations I had with friends just this week. Maybe they sound familiar to you:

"You don't understand," my friend complained. "I've tried everything. She won't listen. She's just a spoiled little brat who's just like her father."

He took another bite of toast and added, "Cher, my brother is a selfish ass who never listens to anything I have to say. Whenever I'm around him, I'm just irritated."

"That's it!" I said to myself, fuming as I listened to my son share yet another hurtful story about his teacher. "I'll take care of it, Michael", I reassured him. As I dried his tears, I picked up the phone and left a voicemail, demanding an immediate meeting. I felt my mind begin wandering- plotting and dreaming about the exact nature and methods I would use to bring about the teacher's eventual demise. "Hmmm..." you may be thinking. "THAT doesn't sound too spiritual." I couldn't agree more. It was anything but.

Conflict. It's hard to get through a single day without it rearing its inevitable head. I don't know what lessons you learned about how to handle it, but my lessons as a little girl who was regularly teased and bullied were clear. I was taught not to take any crap from anyone. I learned to be offended at virtually everything people did that failed to live up to my standard of perfection. I learned to hone my verbal skills to razor-sharp perfection and slash you so clean you wouldn't even bleed if you crossed me or mine. I learned to feel superior to everyone around me, and soon found myself spending my days amazed at how many idiots there were in the world. This then led me to the logical conclusion as an adult that I needed to enlighten those ignorant fools around with me my wisdom- whether they asked for it or not. I learned the only lesson the world had to offer me: Judge. Condemn. Blame. Separate. Find fault. Strike first. Win.

Does this tactic or a variation of it sound familiar to you? If so, you'll want to read on, especially if you have someone in your life who is the source of continual and relentless irritation.

Got conflict? Maybe it's the way they talk to you that drives you mad, always laced with criticism, negativity and blame... maybe you've asked your kids or partner to just put the freakin' dishes in the dishwasher when they're finished eating, only to wake up morning after morning to a sink spilling over as further evidence of their complete disregard for you... or maybe it's just X- the way they treat you, the way they treat someone you love, the silent withholding of kindness, a pattern of outright blatant disregard for your feelings, or an entire history of wounds that all add up to a familiar, gnawing knot in your stomach at the thought of even being in the same room with them. Only you know what "it" is. And only you can resolve "it", if you will only but consider the remote possibility that maybe- just maybe- it's not them at all. It's you. It was always you. It will always be you. It's me. It was always me. It will always be me. When it comes to resolving conflict, there is no greater insight you can have than to understand a simple truth found in two simple words: **It's me.**

So now what? Does this mean that we allow people to walk all over us, mistreat us, say unkind words and treat us like a doormat? Hardly. It means that we begin with the simple understanding that if we want to end any and all conflict in our lives, it begins with me. It begins with you. Of course, the next logical step is that you willingly throw out virtually EVERYTHING the world taught you about how to resolve conflict and become willing to see conflict from a spiritual perspective. This is not a small paradigm shift I'm talking about. This is nothing short of a major mental revolution that will permanently alter the outcome of any conflict you're currently creating. And the outcome is guaranteed: 100% peace.

Remember the conflict I shared about my son's teacher? I used the exact process you're about to read to transform what would have been the creation of an absolute nightmare to the creation of an absolute miracle. The process goes something like this:

1. Acknowledge that there is someone in your life quietly driving you mad. Feel it. Roll around in it. Get in touch with how negative and angry you feel.

2. Consider the possibility that whatever you dislike or judge in them is simply a projection of something about you that you also dislike or judge. You'll want to resist this part, but do it anyway.

3. Get tough. Admit that although you may not know what it is, you must have had some part, however small, in attracting and creating whatever circumstance you find yourself in. (This is the most difficult part for most of us because we've been conditioned for blame and finger pointing. This can take you a moment or years to complete, depending on your level of consciousness.)

4. Get ready to resolve to evolve. Ask yourself the hard questions no one really wants to ask: "What did I do, say or think that helped create this mess?" "What spiritual quality is seeking to emerge in me?" "What quality in me needs to die?" James Allen writes, "*The person who does not shrink from self-crucifixion can never fail to accomplish the object upon which their heart is set.*" Be a spiritual warrior, relentless in pursuit of the answers that are within you.

5. Own it all. Be willing to release everything and anything about you that contributed to the conflict. Say goodbye to judgment, anger, blame, condemnation, jealousy, you name it. If you still don't know what to release, ask God to enlighten you. He always delivers. If you can't hear Spirit talking, ask an honest friend who won't blow smoke up your skirt to help you see what you can't see about yourself. Listen to your friend without being defensive and assume that whatever they're telling you about you is probably spot on. Then go ahead and grieve for a while about how blind you've been. Dry your tears, forgive yourself, and proceed to the next step.

6. Prepare to let go. Get mentally ready to let go of your need for the other person to change anything about themselves. Resolve that you will not ask the other to change a thing- absolutely freakin' nothing. Sound crazy? Maybe. But I'll tell you what's even crazier- expecting someone to change their behavior so that you can feel OK. Now THAT'S crazy. Worse yet, if they don't change, you're stuck. And who wants to be stuck? Instead, I recommend actually convincing yourself prior to the meeting that you expect ZERO change on the part of the other person. It's actually genius because they're not changing anyway, so you're simply agreeing to what is. Besides, your intention in this meeting is not to change them. It's to change you. They are your wonderful teacher and aren't required to do anything for this situation to completely transform itself.

7. Go into meditation or prayer and thank God over and over for this amazing teacher that you attracted for the sole purpose of evolving you to a higher and more loving state of being.

8. Meet. When you see your teacher, talk only of your part in the conflict and your plans to release your contributing behavior in the future. At this point, the most amazing thing will happen. The other person will almost always share with you what an ass they've been too. (No guarantee, mind you... but even if they don't own their part, who cares? It's not about them anyway.) Thank them profusely for giving you such an amazing gift so that you may grow in love and wisdom. When they tell you you're crazy, laugh and agree with them.

9. Sit back, relax, and watch your relationship transform itself from angry and toxic into loving and accepting. Know that from this moment on, no matter what conflict you find yourself in, it's about you. It was always about you. It will always be about you.

    I leave you with this beautiful thought by James Allen: *"As a being of power, intelligence and love, you are the lord of your own thoughts and hold the key to every situation, containing within yourself that transforming and regenerative agency by which you make yourself what you will...as a progressive and evolving being, you are where you are so that you may learn and grow; and as you learn, the spiritual lesson which any circumstance contains for you passes away, giving rise to new circumstances containing new lessons..."* James Allen

Cheri J. Najor, MSW, CSW

For the past 25 years, Cheri has lived her passion and life's mission as the owner and founder of The Center for Peak Performance; a training and communications company that helps people transform their lives and business through the power of conscious communication. As a licensed therapist, speaker and writer, Cheri helps people use the power of language to create healthy, positive relationships with themselves and others. Cheri offers award-winning personal and professional growth seminars and keynote speaking on topics such as Emotional Intelligence, Resolving Conflict, Stress Management, Difficult Discussions and Negotiation.

To reach Cheri, send an e-mail to cheri@centerforpeakperformance.com or visit her website at www.centerforpeakperformance.com.

Endorsement for Kathryn Orford

"If you're ready to let go of limiting beliefs and behaviors that hold you back from being all you can be, I highly recommend you read Kathryn's chapter called "Biggest Nightmare or Biggest Gift". Kathryn is the real deal. She walks her talk, and is such an inspiration to everyone she comes into contact with. Kathryn makes her dreams a reality, and she's a master at teaching people how to do likewise.   So what are you waiting for? Find a cosy corner and start changing your life for the better today!"

- Sam Cawthorn, International Speaker
CEO of Empowering Enterprises
Young Australian of the Year 2009

Chapter 5

Biggest Nightmare or Biggest Gift?

By Kathryn Orford ~ The Confidence Coach. Author, Speaker and Trainer

Use your Smart Phone to watch an Overview of this Chapter.
QR Readers are a free app. Just search for one in your App Store

Life won't always turn out like you hoped it would.
Caught in disappointment, it's hard to see the good.
First you ask why, then shake your fists at the sky.
Finally you cry and you make it to the other side

Bitter or better- the choice is up to you.
Bitter or better, what's it gonna be?
Bitter or better, what you gonna do?
Bitter or better- the choice is up to you.

A very wise man once said these words to me:
'there's no greater teacher than adversity.
First you ask why then shake your fists at the sky.
Finally you cry and you make it to the other side

Lyrics to *"Bitter or Better"* by Jana Stanfield

On 14th April 1978, on a warm Easter Saturday afternoon in Sydney Australia, I married for all the wrong reasons. Since I had just gotten out of my first serious relationship, this marriage was clearly the result of a re-bound relationship. Needless to say it didn't last. I was married at 23 but divorced by the age of 25.

It wasn't until much later on that I discovered that our Pre frontal cortex is a work in progress until we are about 25 years old. This is the part of our brain that enables us to think things through in a logical manner and helps us determine the consequences of our actions. Personally, I know that by the time I was 25 years old, I had a slightly better idea of who I was and who I wanted to spend my time around than when I was 16, or even 21. For precisely that reason, my teenage daughter won't have access to her Gold Shares until she turns 25. Hopefully by then she'll be mature enough to use it wisely and not to blow the whole lot in one foul swoop! If not, I guess she'll learn valuable life lessons.

But I've digressed from my story, so... Now fast forward from my mid 20s to my early 30's. I had just embarked on my personal development journey, learning Transcendental Meditation, reading Louise Hay's legendary best seller, You can heal your life, along with Shakti Gawain's two books, Living in the Light and Creative Visualization.

During this transitional time, a friend introduced me to an extremely charismatic man training to be a facilitator with Robert Kiyosaki. We began dating, and it seemed natural that I would attend '$ and U', one of the courses that Kiyosaki was facilitating. This course was the beginning of my interest in Robert Kiyosaki's courses and it was the first of many more courses that I attended. I was present for courses like 'Creating Wealth' and 'Powerful Presentations'; suddenly a whole new world opened up and I began to thrive on my new found skills and awareness. I also thought I'd met the "man of my dreams," but unfortunately, he actually turned out to be my "Biggest Nightmare!"

Not only did Greg cheat on me and blatantly lie to my face when I confronted him about it, he also married the "other women" within three months of dumping me. To say I was heart-broken was a gross understatement. It felt as though he had ripped my heart out of my chest, thrown it onto the ground and stomped all over it.

At that stage, I didn't know that I was adopted, so his actions triggered my "abandonment issues" big time! I felt completely unlovable and worthless. To make matters worse, Greg, his new wife and I were enrolled in a six-month course called 'Training to Train' with Stephanie Burns! In a disturbing quirk of fate, I was in their study group! Talk about masochistic! Looking back, I don't know why I didn't ask to be switched to another group; perhaps a sick part of me still wanted to be part of Greg's inner circle. Not surprisingly, every time I saw them together it felt as if my heart was being battered and bruised all over again. Somehow I managed to complete the course. It wasn't long after that, however, that I spiraled down into the deepest darkest depression.

Every ounce of my "I'm not good enough demons" had reared their ugly heads and were literally strangling me! Day by day, I'd gear up with my suit of armor and pretend everything was fine but deep down inside, I could feel my life force draining from me. One moment I was a confident vivacious young woman in her early 30's, full of life and positive anticipation, running an incredibly successful School of Performing Arts. Then suddenly, the next moment, I felt totally worthless. My self-esteem plummeted. I began to doubt my ability to do anything. I couldn't choreograph or dance well, or even think coherently for too long. I felt like a complete failure!

I remember one day while walking out into my back garden, all I could see were caterpillars and snails eating the flowers and leaves. My previous "rose colored glasses" approach to life had disappeared, only to be replaced by a "murky pair of black lenses." It was as if the firm ground that I'd previously stood on had turned into quicksand. Every day I slipped deeper and deeper below the surface until I could barely breathe. My world became very dark and lonely. The scariest thing by far was when I turned on music and felt nothing. Music had given me such joy in the past, and developing choreography was how I connected with my essence and expressed my true spirit- but those exquisite feelings had totally disappeared, only to be replaced by feelings of complete apathy and NUMBNESS!

At one point, I got to the stage where I didn't want to get out of bed. When I did get out of bed, I would be overwhelmed by "anxiety attacks" at the thought of having to teach my dance classes.

Although close friends and family kept telling me to look for the light at the end of the tunnel, I assure you, there was no light; it was pitch black! Unfortunately, their well-meaning comments just made me feel even more isolated.

After soldiering on for several months, the pain became unbearable altogether. I decided I couldn't stand it anymore, so it was time for me to "check out" and commit suicide. That afternoon, I went to visit my parents for the final time and when I left, I remember looking back at their front door and telepathically sending them a message saying "thank you and please forgive me."

Somehow, I mustered up enough energy to teach my dance classes for the day. My last class was one of my favorites—my beautiful 10 year olds' Competition Team. Somehow I got through their class, and as they started leaving the studio I also telepathically sent them a message, saying "thank you for all the joy you've brought me, please forgive me and please keep dancing."

As the remaining students were disappearing out the door, I fell heavily on the polished wooden floor and sobbed deeply. A few students heard my cries and rushed back to see what was wrong. I reassured them by saying something like "oh I'll be okay; I'm just having a tough time in my private life," before ushering them quickly back out the door.

Somehow despite my agony, I managed to drive home. I went straight to my bathroom to find the anti-depressants I planned to pour down my throat but thankfully, I couldn't find the bottle. In fact I couldn't even find the script. You see I'd never planned on taking them. I'd only really gone to the doctors to appease my mother, who became worried when I suffered anxiety attacks and wouldn't leave my bed. I continued rifling through the bathroom cupboards and drawers trying to find something that would do the trick, but since I'd always preferred homeopathic to traditional medicine, I couldn't find anything remotely capable of killing me. The entire situation would have been comical had I not been on the verge of suicide.

So once again I fell in a heap on the cold bathroom tiles sobbing hysterically. The critical voice in my head reared its ugly self, berating me mercilessly: "you're so pathetic!" "You can't even organize your own suicide properly!"

I was curled up in a fetal position on those cold bathroom tiles, rocking myself back and forth when the phone rang. There was no way I was about to get off the floor and answer it, so I let it ring out. But it rang again, and again. The third time the phone rang, a gentler voice inside of me said "get up and answer it." I think I was worried that something bad might have happened to my mum or dad. So I slowly unfolded my wasted body and picked up the phone just before it rang out for the third time. I thought perhaps my mum or dad was calling, but as it turned out, one of my beautiful students' mothers was on the line.

She said uncertainly, "Are you okay?" When her daughter had come home from class, she'd told her mother how upset I was. I responded, "no, but I will be." And in that instant she read between the lines and said "I'm in the middle of cooking dinner, but I want you to promise me you won't do anything? I'll be there in 20 mins." I knew the only way to end the call was to agree; however, I had no intention of keeping my promise. All I wanted to do was get off the phone and come up with Plan B.

I realized I'd have to move quickly and leave the house before she arrived. As I grabbed the car keys and walked towards the front door I remember saying to myself, "oh well, you'll have to drive your car off a cliff. I hope you can get that right, and not end up a paraplegic!"

Much to my surprise, just as I was about to open the front door, someone rang the doorbell. Standing there was another one of my student's parents, with a huge bouquet of beautiful flowers in her arms. She said "We know you're going through a rough time at the moment, so we want you to know how much we love you."

At that precise moment I remembered an analogy Robert Kiyosaki had shared with us in the first Personal Development Course I'd attended, "$ & U." He said that in life when we're off track, we'll often get a tap on the shoulder to alert us. If we ignore the first tap, the second one will be much harder. And if we don't listen to that one, next thing we know, we are flat on our backs with the smell of diesel filling our lungs and the Mack Truck tread marks across our body, wondering what the f— hit us!

As I stood dumbfounded in my doorway with the flowers in my arms, I thought "maybe I'm not meant to go after all? I've just received two taps on the shoulder. Greg doesn't love you, but lots of other people do, so maybe it's time for you to learn to love yourself from the inside out instead of constantly searching for outside acknowledgement that you're okay."

In that very moment I made a pledge to myself: I promised that I would never feel that bad about myself ever again. I would never allow anyone to rob me of my self-esteem. When I made that pledge, the real work began. Was it easy? Gosh no! Was it worth it? Absolutely!

I now know that what I thought was my biggest nightmare, actually turned out to be my "biggest gift."

Some would say I suffered a nervous breakdown. But I call it my "Break Down to Breakthrough" to the real me! In that moment that I chose life, I chose to build myself up, brick by brick, day by day; to be the confident, happy Mark 2 version of the woman that I am today! Honestly, I wouldn't change a thing!

It's been an amazing journey so far. Since my "Breakthrough Moment" 23 years ago, I have immersed myself in learning everything I can about how to feel great about myself. I've had the pleasure of studying with the world's leading authorities on self-esteem, self-belief and human potential. I now consider myself to be one of them.

My "tool kit" is a veritable smorgasbord of techniques, mindsets and beliefs that have certainly worked for me, and they can work for you too. So enough about me; let's get started.

The Beginning

As that famous song from The Sound of Music goes, "Let's start at the very beginning, a very good place to start."

So what do I mean by that? Well, at the beginning, or when you were born, you had more than enough self-esteem and self-worth to last a lifetime.

Think about it—have you ever seen a new-born child displaying self-loathing, hatred or negativity? Of course not! As tiny babies, we know how special and unique we are, and that all our needs are important.

When we were hungry, we let the world know; when we were tired, we broadcasted it to the nation; and when we were wet and needed a clean nappy, we communicated that loud and clear because we knew our needs were important!

We've all witnessed the amazing effect that babies and young animals have on the people around them. They bring out our best qualities as human beings, and they have the capacity to melt even the hardest heart!

Why is that? Well I think it's because they are incredibly innocent, pure and vulnerable. Being around babies rekindles something deep within us; we reconnect with the fact that we were once that exquisite and whole!

So what happened? How did we lose those feelings of self-acceptance, self- worth, joy, curiosity and positive anticipation?

Those wonderful newborn feelings started to erode sometime after we learnt how to walk. How and when it happened will be different for each of us, but ultimately, somewhere along the line, we received "feedback" from someone around us that something we did or said was "not OK"! That negation came as a huge shock!

Up until then, everything we did as young babies was not only acceptable, it was fabulous! We received encouragement and acknowledgement for every little move and sound we made.

Stop and think about it. When a small child falls over attempting to take those first few shaky steps, have you ever heard a family member scream "Stand up and do it again you silly idiot!" Of course not! We encourage babies in a soft loving voice to get up and have another go, and we applaud like crazy when they do something new for the first time!

As tiny babies we could do no wrong. We stuck our finger up our nose and they thought we were cute. When we farted, they laughed. So as I said before, we experienced a huge shock when we received feedback for the first time that we weren't perfect.

The analogy I use is that when we were born, we had an infinite amount of balloons, and those balloons represented our self-esteem.

EXERCISE: SELF ESTEEM BALLOONS

Take a moment now to choose a color or perhaps several colors that represent the "essence" of who you are. Imagine a balloon that color in front of you right now and then imagine someone clicking their fingers, and that balloon magically multiplies to fill the room you're in. As the balloons continue to multiply, see them filling your entire house or building. See them floating out of the windows and doors and down the street. Imagine standing on the rooftop of your house or building, turning a complete 360 degrees, and for as far as your eyes can see and beyond, you see your multiplying balloons. THAT'S HOW MUCH SELF ESTEEM YOU WERE BORN WITH!

So what happened?

As I mentioned before, somewhere between 1 – 2 years old, you received your first negative feedback. Your parents might have scolded, "That's naughty, don't do that," or a child might have flicked sand in your eyes in the sandpit. Or perhaps a jealous older sibling pushed you over when mum or dad left the room. Whatever it was for you, your brain was not developed enough to realize that the negative comment or action was about an action that you were doing.

Perhaps that first negative experience had nothing to do with you, and was purely fueled by someone else's feelings of inadequacy. For example, an older sibling may have been jealous of the newest addition to the family. Whatever the experience or feedback, you personalized it and decided that you must be flawed in some way; that came as a terrible shock.

That shock popped one or more of your balloons and created the foundation for self-doubt. We're neurologically wired to look for evidence to support our feelings so chances are, you started looking for evidence that you weren't so perfect after all and unfortunately, you probably found plenty of it.

Have you heard of Jack Canfield? He co-wrote the Chicken Soup for the Soul Books, and was also featured in the book (and movie) The Secret. In 1982 Jack researched how many positive and how many negative comments a young child in pre-school receives each day. He found that on average they received 460 negative or critical comments and only 75 positive or supportive comments. Now that's both scary and very revealing!

So in one week, that's 3,220 negative comments against 525 positive ones.

In a month that, adds up to 14,260 negative comments and 2,325 positive ones. Over a year that adds up to a whopping 171,120 negative comments and only 27,900 positive ones. That's a lot of balloons being popped!! Think about what a devastating effect all those negations or popped balloons have on our self-esteem! And of course when we went to school the pattern continued. So over 6 years that adds up to 102 million 6,720 negative comments.

Is it any wonder that by the time we reach the age of 8, we feel flawed, inadequate, and "not good enough?", and have very active critical voices inside our heads?

You could get angry and say "How could my parents have done this to me?" But you know what, I'm guessing your parents were just doing the best they could with the knowledge and skills they had available to them. And let's face it; they probably based their parenting style on how they were parented. Moreover, their parents probably based their parenting style on how they were parented. And so it goes!

EXERCISE: BUILD YOUR SELF ESTEEM BANK

Remember the analogy I used earlier about having an infinite amount of balloons when we are born that represent our self-esteem? Well now I'd like you to imagine that you have a "Bank Account." No, not a traditional bank account filled with money, but an Emotional Self-Esteem Account that withdraws or accrues your self-esteem and self-worth.

Every time you put yourself down or do something that negates who you are, you are making a withdrawal from your Self-Esteem Account. On the flip side, every time you compliment yourself or celebrate a win, you are depositing self-esteem and self-worth into your account.

Whilst some of you might feel that there isn't much in your account right now or that you might even be operating from an overdraft, the great news is that you can change that right now by simply acknowledging that you are ready and willing to change.

Chances are, you've probably been tough on yourself up until now, so find ways every day to make a deposit, and watch your balance grow. Alternatively, returning to my balloon analogy, blow up a balloon to celebrate your unique self. If you do that every day for 30 days, can you imagine how many more self-worth balloons and self-esteem deposits you will have? You can't help but feel better about yourself.

The great news is that you're now in a position to BREAK THAT CYCLE AND CLAIM BACK YOUR SELF ESTEEM AND SELF WORTH FOR GOOD!

RE-PROGRAM YOUR NEGATIVE SELF TALK

If you are like most of the population, you probably have some negative self talk going on inside your head. That nagging voice that puts you down when you get stressed or stuff up, or you feel out of your depths. You know, the one that tells you that you aren't good enough, clever enough, pretty enough, handsome enough et cetera. Most of us have a bottom line belief that "I'm not good enough".

That voice can have a devastating effect on how we feel about ourselves.

The really cool thing is that neurons that fire together, wire together. So whilst that negative voice is wired to rear its ugly head, you can set about re-wiring it, by creating new neurological pathways.

It takes practice, but hey what have you got to lose? Just the critical voice that puts you down!

Scan the QR Code below to take you to a video of me demonstrating how to Re-Program your Negative Self Talk.

For those of you that don't have access to a Smart Phone, here are 4 ways to re-program your negative self talk:

- Change the tone: From critical to silly or sexy. Imagine saying it like Donald Duck, and it will totally change the impact- in fact it will probably make you laugh!

- Change the volume. Imagine hitting the mute button on a remote control or reaching up and turning down the volume.

- Drown it out. Say something like "Out of here, I don't need you anymore!"

- Add a positive onto the end of the negative by using a Y.U.I. It's an acronym I've come up with. In Australia when we do a U turn, we refer to is as "chucking a YUI." And just like when you do a U turn in a car, adding one of these words on to the end of a negative will take your thought process in the opposite direction.

Y = Yet
U = Up until now
I = In the past.

So for example if you say:

'I can't do that...' add "Yet." What does that tell you? It presupposes that you will be able to do it if you persevere.

'My boss never chooses me to pitch to a new client...'add "Up until Now"

'Every time I go for a promotion I don't get it...'add "In the past", which puts the negative though in the past where it belongs.

Take a moment now to experiment. You've probably spent many years perfecting that negative voice, so it will take time and effort to change it. Nonetheless, I'm living proof that it is possible. Speaking from personal experience, it's very liberating when at last the negative voice is replaced with your own personal cheer squad that is supportive and encouraging! Occasionally if I get stressed and a negative thought does sneak in, a positive response kicks in automatically without me doing a thing. Because neurons that fire together, wire together.

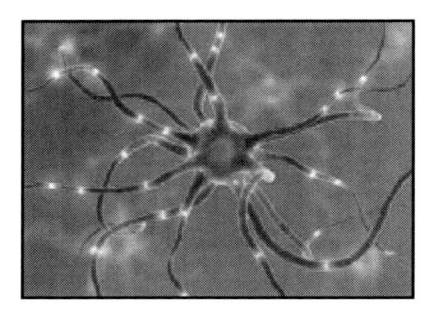

Here you can see dendrites connecting and creating new neural pathways
So stay persistent and create your own cheer squad in your head!!

EXERCISE ~ Re-connecting with your inner child

That tiny little person still lives inside your adult body. And they're waiting patiently for you to re-connect with them. Just like the lone piece of luggage at the baggage carousel at the airport, going round and round, waiting for someone to claim it: your inner child is buried deep inside of you just waiting for the day that you'll finally notice them! And perhaps today is that day? So:

~ Find a favorite picture of yourself as a baby aged between 6 – 18 months old.

~ Look into that beautiful baby's eyes. Spend time re-connecting with the joy, curiosity and positive anticipation that emanates from their very being!

~ Now look into your tiny child's eyes and apologize for not being there for him/her lately. And re-commit to nurturing them and taking good care of them from this day on.

~ Put your picture up in your bedroom or bathroom.

~ As you start each day, look into your tiny child's eyes and assure them that you're there for them; that you're going to treat them with the love and respect that they deserve.

~ You might also like to carry a copy of your picture in your wallet as a reminder for your adult self as you go about your day.

~ If you forget and fall back into old patterns of behavior that don't honor that little child, apologize and re-commit to doing better tomorrow.

REFLECTION TIME

How was this exercise for you? What realizations have you had since doing this exercise?

That tiny child still lives inside our adult body, so find fun ways to re-connect with them and honor their needs. Do something spontaneous and a little crazy at least once a week, preferably once a day. And then write down in your journal how it made you feel.

RE-CAP

When you were born you knew how special and unique you were and that your needs were important. You had more than enough self-esteem and self-worth to last a lifetime. Negative comments and feedback eroded your sense of self, but it's time right now to reclaim what is rightfully yours and build your Self-Esteem Bank on a daily basis. You are not your behaviors. You learnt them from everyone around you.

Who you are is a magnificent human being, overflowing with potential!

Every day we're faced with situations that we can be bitter about, or alternatively choose to learn from and to be better for the experience. The choice is yours!

I know personally, what I thought was my Biggest Nightmare turned out to be my Biggest Gift. And as painful as that period of my life was, I wouldn't change a thing! Life is full of paradoxes. We need to have experienced sadness and pain to truly recognize and appreciate joy; confusion to experience clarity; and self loathing to move to a place of self love and self worth.

IN CLOSING

I've shared my story in the hope that it inspires you to become who you really are. I've provided you with some tools and techniques that certainly worked for me and that can work for you too! Have fun learning to love yourself from the inside out and building your Self Esteem Bank exponentially.

You'll find lots of free resources, including a Self Esteem Evaluation Form, on my website: www.theconfidencecoach.net.au

Do email me at the address below with any questions or feedback about this chapter:
kathryn@theconfidencecoach.net.au

Kathryn Orford

Known as The Confidence Coach, Kathryn has spent the last 35 years empowering people to believe in themselves and their abilities. She has trained with the world's leading experts in human behavior and potential. And nothing light's her up more than witnessing her clients produce results they had only previously dreamt of. For many years Kathryn ran a highly successful School of Performing Arts and has ex-students scattered around the world performing in movies, musicals, dance companies, operas etc....

She also ran Self Esteem and Life Skills Programs for young people. These days Kathryn is in demand as a Speaker, Peak Performance Coach and Trainer and specializes in working with athletes, performers, personal trainers and sales people. In fact anyone interested in freeing themselves of their limiting beliefs so they can create the life they dream of! She is also the Visionary and Goddess at GODDESSES~UNITE GLOBAL COMMUNITY on Facebook and runs "Awaken your Goddess" in Hawaii.

www.theconfidencecoach.net

kathrynbelleorford@gmail.com

Endorsement for Kim Rinaldi-Robey

"I have known Kim for many years. One of the things I have always known is....That Kim has perseverance with a great attitude. Until I read what she said in this book I had no idea the level of tough times she had gone through...and kept going strong. When you read her story you will also see the thread that kept her going to the level of success she has today. It is something you too can learn and incorporate no matter where you are in life. Check this book out!"

- Mark J. Ryan
www.MarkJRyan.com

Chapter 6
No Room for Fear

They say everyone has a story. I believe that this is probably true. That being said, I would imagine that there is a really strong chance that the story that I am about to share with you is one you have heard before. Oh sure, the names of the places and people will have been changed, but my story is bound to be a repeat performance of something you have already heard.

Over the years, I have listened to and read more stories than I can count. Some of them were funny, some sad and many were very thought-provoking. Even at times when many of the stories that I read were similar to others I had already heard, one would come along that would blind-side me. There would be something different about a story that would reach out and touch some of my deepest stored emotions; emotions that I had stored very deeply, and that I generally avoided digging up and rehashing. You know the ones I mean; the emotions that appear easier to stuff down than to deal with. It was these stories that were sprinkled in the mix of my experiences that would keep running through my mind, forcing me to rethink, reevaluate, reconnect with my God and eventually create change in my world.

I am eternally grateful for the changes that I have made. Out of this gratitude, I share my story with you. I do not believe in accidents. If you were inclined to pick up this book, then turn to this page and make some time to read this chapter - there is a reason! Everything that I have been through on my journey has served a purpose and maybe, just maybe, part of that purpose is to help someone else as they search for answers on their own path.

When I was in my early thirties, I would imagine that my life seemed "normal" from the outside looking in. I had been married since I was nineteen. We had two young children, a house, and two dogs. Normal. It's funny how even when things are unraveling at the speed of light, we keep working diligently to keep up appearances. My life experiences up to that point had formed an impression on me of what my role in this life was. This image was based on what I had been taught over the years. The thought of deviation from the course I was guided along was something that I seldom dared to entertain; I lived daily playing out my role in life. Was I happy? Of course! I was a good wife, a great mother, a good daughter, sister, etc. I took care of everyone... Everyone except me I guess. If I was good at all these things, then I must have been happy, right? Maybe you know somebody in a similar stage of life?

I really can't tell you that there was one monumental turning point in my life; there was no single defining moment where it all suddenly made sense. However, there are a few significant moments that stand out in my mind. Bankruptcy was the first change that "rocked my world" to the point that others noticed. Others in my life had gone bankrupt before. I didn't think poorly of them, but there was something to be said for toughing it out and managing to evade bankruptcy. Suddenly finding myself in these shoes made for many a sleepless night. The realization that I could not control life the way I thought I was able to proved to be unnerving, to say the least. I spent many hours thinking about who I wanted to be and what I wanted my life to be like. This was new to me as prior to this, my thoughts had more to do with the expectations others had of me. I started realizing that I was not happy. It was an unhappiness that went beyond the circumstances of the moment. With life in general, there were areas where I was just plain unsatisfied. There were certainly happy times and there were people that I loved in my life, but SOMETHING was missing. Maybe you know somebody who has felt this way before.

Rewind to about a year earlier. Although I had suffered migraine headaches for several years, they had become so frequent that they now affected me on a daily basis. No surprise there, right? I had the kind of migraines that included tunnel vision and nausea. I remember being at the mall with my children and having to sit down for a short while because I could only see a narrow path directly in front of me. I was truly afraid that I would black out and no one would be there to take care of the kids and make sure they didn't wander off. Another day I remember riding a bike with my daughter in her Cookie Monster carrier on the back. I had stopped at a stop sign when everything started going fuzzy on me. Two men in a car behind us jumped out and grabbed the bike keeping me from dumping my child on the street. We got through those days, but boy, do I remember the chaos my migraines would cause.

I had a friend who kept telling me about essential oils and how her family was using them for their health issues. I thought, "You have got to be kidding me". After a year and a half of her sharing this information with me regularly, she asked me about my migraines during a telephone conversation. I told her that I had them daily. My options were to deal with the pain or take my medicine that made my stomach upset. By the end of the phone call I had agreed to try her oils. I'm not even sure why I chose to give in on that day, but she had pressed for over a year and a half - I guess I had just resisted long enough. My logic was that if I tried them, then maybe she would be able to move on to telling others about them but finally drop them from our conversations. Surely they wouldn't work, but I would humor her. I seriously thought that she either didn't know what a migraine was, or that she had been sold a bag of goods herself; maybe a little of both. I gave the oils a shot, and I was utterly shocked at the following days' events. When my migraine started and I applied the oil just as she had told me to, it was a matter of a couple of minutes and the symptoms were GONE. Figuring that it was a fluke, I remained very skeptical of these oils even though there were repeated occasions when I would follow the same procedure and my migraines would vanish. From there, I figured that oils must be good for headaches but that's about it.

Even with my cynicism, I started to address my children's asthma and had amazing results there as well. My son was eleven at the time and he came to my room in the middle of the night. He said "Mom, I'm in trouble". He was in a full blown asthma attack that seemed to come out of nowhere. I had researched essential oils and had chosen one specific blend that contained 13 essential oils that I thought would be supportive while dealing with asthma. I told my son "let me get the oil. If they don't work really fast then I will get your inhalers okay?" He agreed with a nod of his head. Joel was on two different inhalers at that time. I grabbed the oils and put a few drops in the palm of my hand. I rotated the puddle of oil around with my fingertips and applied them to his chest. I applied them to his feet. I had no idea where the reflex points were for his bronchial tubes, but I applied the oils on his feet nonetheless. Then my hands appeared dry but I cupped them and held them up in front of him. I said "just breathe as much as you can Joel". Joel lay down at the foot of my bed. I rested my head on my pillow while I played back in my mind which inhalers were Joel's and which ones were Beth's, what one went first and how long I had to wait to do the second one... Suddenly, I realized Joel was sound asleep. The asthma attack had passed completely and he was snoring at the foot of my bed. Only a few minutes had passed. Come to think of it, he never even got scared or started crying, which always made the attacks worse. He remained calm through the whole process. All at once I knew in my heart that these oils were a gift in my life. I had loved finding a way to deal with my own pain but now it was different. Now these "crazy little oils", as I used to refer to them, had made a difference in my children's lives. They were no longer crazy - they were a blessing. Isn't it funny how your attitude towards things changes when they have an impact on your children? Maybe you can relate?

Now I was at a cross roads. Money was beyond tight. Oils cost money. What to do? I had signed up as a "distributor" for Young Living Essential Oils but had absolutely NO intention of working the business. I had been a salesman's daughter and held enough sales positions over the years, but I had no desire to be a salesperson. I signed up so that I could get wholesale prices - plain and simple. But now I found myself experiencing a new world with these oils and feeling compelled to share this information with everyone. That little inner voice that we so often like to ignore was screaming at me; the light-bulb went off!

If I had endless praises for these oils, and I needed to make enough to cover the cost of my new habit - maybe I could look into the business side and make some money by actually building an oils business! It couldn't hurt, right? I spent that evening on the phone with two of the girls that had introduced me to oils. The first one, who I originally thought was out of her mind, told me that I would need to talk to her sister as she did not work the business side of the oils. Imagine that? This friend had talked to me endlessly about these oils for over a year and a half but she "didn't work the business side". I knew who her sister was but did not know her personally. I called her and told her to just shoot straight with me. How much are you making?" She shared with me that at that time she would make two to three hundred dollars on a good month. That was the answer I was looking for. Let me make more than enough for any oils and products that I believed my family needed and I would be content. I just couldn't go without oils and I couldn't reach into my pocket and create another expense. We agreed to partner up, put 6 months into building this business and see what happened. Both of us had thrown away six months on far less worthy ventures before. At the end of six months if it wasn't working out, no harm done.

We started by jumping into a local health event. I knew very little about oils at the time but I knew trade shows from having worked around them with my father since I was a young teenager. I looked around the room at all of the vendors doing their thing. I watched the people and how honestly interested they were, deeply involved in conversation at the different booths. I turned to my business partner and said "We can do this, and we don't have to wait for someone else to book a fair. We can book our own." From there we booked our own health events in neighboring cities. Immediately we came to realize there were so many other people, many mothers, who had the same questions we had had in the beginning. We would work our Young Living booth at our event and promote a follow up gathering at a local space for them to come and spend an evening learning more and having their questions answered. We were not just building business but we were building relationships with great people-and we were having a ball! The business began to really take off.

Back to my bankruptcy -

I will never forget sitting in the attorney's office. Just being in that office was so far beyond my comfort zone. We were going over the amount of income that was coming into the house. I was running an in-home daycare center at the time, and I told him that I had also been building a network marketing business for the past year or so and was looking forward to that growing in the future. I was wounded when the attorney looked pompously across the desk and said, "You might want to consider getting a real job dear". A "real job"? A REAL JOB?!?! My blood was boiling instantly. I wasn't sure if I was more hurt or angry but there was definitely a crazy strong emotion that was causing my eyes to well up. However, I took his condescending remark on the chin and made no reply. This man had no idea how I spent my days. He had no idea that I got up everyday around five a.m., let the dogs out, worked my business online, got ready for a full day of daycare, home schooled two children, fixed dinner for four, and many nights either headed back out to work my oils business or take my daughter to dance classes or just grab the weekly groceries, before managing to fall back into bed somewhere around 11p.m.. I accomplished more than many by noon everyday yet I didn't have the backbone to confidently respond to this man (whose time I was paying for, by the way). Over the years I have often thought of sending him a copy of my check and telling him how happy I am that I didn't take his advice; but what good would that do? It was very insulting at the time, but looking back I can see how just that one statement by a man I might have spent a few hours of my entire lifetime with made me acutely aware that I was on a path that I planned to stay on. There was a purpose to what I was doing and it meant something to me; something not every person would understand, but something I needed to follow through with.

The bankruptcy came to pass and more life changes closely followed. Six months after filing for bankruptcy we went back to court to start divorce proceedings to end a fifteen year marriage. It was ugly- aren't they all? I pulled in support from the few places I could get it. I found myself a single mom working from home. My daycare had closed a year ahead of schedule. Bankrupt and no child support. I eventually went to social services for 4 months of "food stamps", as they used to be called. I was making money with my oils business but not enough to cover everything just yet. Some people keep their home through bankruptcy but that was not the case for us. So there I sat in a home that wouldn't be mine for much longer and no credit to go buy or rent anything. We somehow (no accidents, remember) came across an old trailer that was on a lake in Central New York. I spoke with the landlord and explained my situation. He was willing to take a chance on us. Not only could we move in, but we got to bring the kids' dogs with us. We were far from living large but we had all that we needed. It was embarrassing and unsettling to go to a stranger and ask for help but I learned that when you need someone to give you a chance, when you need just one person to believe in you - the right person will show up.

There is ALWAYS a choice

Life had certainly taken a few crazy turns and held some immense potholes in the road, but my life had actually just begun changing. There were some very turbulent times over those years. I was stuck in a pattern of believing that life was happening to me - it was years later that I realized that even the most difficult aspects in life were happening for me. Blessings are often so well disguised at their very start that they are completely beyond recognition. Repeatedly, friends and coworkers would ask me "how are you doing this?" or tell me "you're moving really fast" and those comments really didn't make much sense to me at the time. What choice did I have? To me, my life was about as low as it was going to get. I used to think that I had no choice but to make the moves I was making. "I had no choice" kept ringing through my mind. No choice, no choice...

I went to a training program that was so impressionable that I don't believe I will ever forget it. It was supposed to be about essential oils and I'm sure a portion of it was. The part that had a profound effect on me was when the speaker spoke about not letting outside influences determine where you are headed and what is important to you. She then sang a song that she had written. I can't for the life of me remember the song, but I do remember the main theme: "Follow Your Heart". I had the ability to contain my emotions in public quite well at that point. But that song; something about it... I fell apart. Sitting toward the front of the room, I could not get out without causing a scene so I just put my head down and the tears rolled. Following my heart, making choices, sowing so as to reap what I wanted - all of it was becoming abundantly clear.

Now I realize that we always have a choice. My choice then was to either just lie down and die, or to pick up and salvage what I could of my world, make changes to enrich the lives of my children, and build the best possible life I could imagine. For me "lying down and giving up" was not an option so I never even considered it to be a "choice". My two greatest blessings in my life to that point were ten and twelve and they meant everything to me. I simply had to carve out a life and make everything okay again.

I started listening to and reading every self improvement/motivational training I could get my hands on. I had a hunger for this information unlike any I had ever had before. I started putting away little bits of money to be able to travel to different trainings. The Law of Attraction made perfect sense to me. There were those who said that people who taught the Law of Attraction were in one way or another not Godly; it seemed to have somehow threatened a select group that felt that we should only rely on what scriptures tell us- or more precisely, what religion taught us. Even if the message was the same, if the verbiage differed they wouldn't be able to accept it. From the beginning of my journey learning about the Law of Attraction I felt the training was synonymous with reaping what we sow, and that each side of the fence was saying the same thing; just using terms that they were most comfortable with. I repeatedly saw how groups of people would immediately reject anything that they did not understand. If the herd was used to a certain paradigm, then any thought of divergence was feared. This was not just a gentle nervous fear, but more of a shear panic and terror that would immediately take hold. I began listening and watching for where I thought God was leading me and what messages would serve me well, paying more attention to what the message was than to who God had sent it through.

Opportunities started presenting themselves. Life is about change and the changes just kept coming. My character was being stretched. I was asked to participate in a corporate sponsored program where they paid my way and flew me to four cities in five nights to share and teach groups of people. Having never been in an airport by myself before, never rented a car or even been in some of the states I found myself in, this was always a great adventure. I would take these trips once a month for about half of the year. Imagine learning each day just what you are capable of. Seriously, imagine it. Put the book down and close your eyes for a few minutes and think what it would feel like to experience wonderful new feelings and places; to discover an amazingly strong and talented person on the inside that you have never recognized before. Are you brave enough to try this?

Welcome back! Where were we? Changes...

I eventually got remarried. My husband Dell and I added onto the family with a beautiful little boy, Dylan Hunter. We were living in a small apartment when I was pregnant. There just wasn't enough space to put one more person in our home so we started house shopping. Remember that I was the one who had been through bankruptcy. When I lost my home, I had promised myself that I would someday own a home again; that I would own it. I had even announced this vision at a class that I held for local people in my business. When I had shared this with them, there hadn't been a dry eye in the room. It was something that I felt very emotional about and apparently I had been able to share that emotion with them. My husband already owned property and understood how important this was to me. But with bankruptcy on my record, how was I going to pull this one off?

My business had been growing steadily. I had sown all the best seeds and had great faith that whatever was supposed to happen, would. I had a number in my head and after speaking with a mortgage broker, we decided what our top price would be. We looked...and looked. There was one neighborhood in particular that...how should I say this...we stalked. Dell and I would go for a ride and just happen to drive through this neighborhood all the time. Most of the homes on the water were well beyond our price range, but I dreamed none the less. Dell was even better about dreaming. Being a sea captain, he was intent on being near the water if not on it.

One day while driving through the neighborhood we drove past a house and I said "that wasn't for sale yesterday". The house was put on the market that day - Friday. Dell had to work the next day but sent me to go look at the house. Now, when I heard the price I had every intention of going back to Dell and telling him it just wasn't for us. Then I walked through the front door and looked out the full wall window at the beautiful river. It was the month of June and the trees were all perfectly green, the pool was crystal clear and the river twinkled in the sunlight. I knew I might be in trouble here. Next we turned the corner into the kitchen- a kitchen most women would love. On into a family room with more windows looking to the river... I was sold. I really did not want to like the house and I followed the agent through the rest of the house trying in my mind to find something that would be a deal breaker- the PRICE! That was all I had to work with. I went back to Dell and confessed that I loved the house and I was sure he was going to like it. I then reminded him the asking price and how massively far beyond our ceiling it was. That's when my husband said "What would Bob Proctor say?"

Oh, of course, now would be the time to remind me of all the training that I had been drinking in for years. I believed that Bob would tell me to find the house I want, and then find a way to get it. As I write this for you I am thinking of two nights ago when I personally sat with Bob and told him that I was going to share this story with you. He nodded in agreement that that is exactly what he would have told me and smiled that we had made the right choice. So we went together to look at the house again. We contacted the mortgage broker and proceeded forward. I just kept praying that whatever was to our highest good would come to pass, trying to stay unattached to the outcome; wanting this home but being determined that if it wasn't to be, I would trust that something better was coming our way. The house went on the market on Friday and we put in a purchase offer on Sunday. That's right, we had an agent meet us at the office and do the papers on Sunday. I wouldn't say that it went without a glitch but we managed to buy the home. That was four and half years after my bankruptcy. At a time when no one would have ever bet I could have bought anything, we closed on a home well beyond our self imposed limit.

But the story gets better.

We moved into our home on August 5th- my birthday. After a few minutes in the house, I found my husband sitting down on the dock - crying. This neighborhood was where he had been when he was a teenager and he had said "someday I'm going to live here". Not someday I'm going to live in a neighborhood like this but "live HERE". How's that for words having power? God had not only brought us to the neighborhood we loved but we are even on the river in a home we could hardly have dared dream of.

I can't say that life never has chaos. Life is unpredictable. But as I look back on the journey, I know this much is true -"Life does begin at the end of your comfort zone". I know from experience that when you are leaving that comfort zone, you know it. I know that every part of your being tends to wonder if you should just turn around and get back inbounds as fast as humanly possible. I promise you that you will be better off than you ever dreamed if you can just force your way through that fear. So many times over the years I have seen people back down and give up just before the breakthrough moment was about to arrive. If they had any clue that within moments the fear would be a thing of the past, they would never have given up. Maybe you know someone who is almost there. Maybe, just maybe, it's you? If so, there are a few things that might be helpful to remember:

"This too shall pass"

These words would echo in my mind. I would say them to myself each time that it all became overwhelming. It doesn't matter what it is that is going on or how incredibly intense the moment may be - time does not stop and "this too shall pass"; It simply never fails. I would think back often on a day that I spent on a front porch visiting with my grandmother. I was just a teenager at the time. My grandma had broken out with Shingles on the inside. To be more specific she had Shingles behind her eye. It was a serious enough case that her eyeball was protruding out of its socket. I went out on the porch to visit and hopefully encourage Grandma. Alone time with my Grandma was a special treat in and of itself. I don't really remember any other time in my life when she and I visited, just the two of us. I have no idea what I said to her that day. Probably something simple and naive but meant with love, intending for it to bring her some sort of comfort. I do, however, remember the words of this frail little woman. There she was in pain and far more sick than any of us yet realized when I heard her assure herself that "this too shall pass"! What incredible strength. I saw a side of my grandmother that day that I had never seen before, and a vision of her that would serve me well long after that day. This is the memory I would often pull forward when it seemed like I surely was going through things far more difficult than people could understand from the outside looking in. It would remind me that other people have been through tougher spots, and even if my heart was breaking, it would come to pass and someday it would all just be a memory.

While it seemed like life was taking unfair shots at me; like life was happening to me and not for me, there was something else I kept reminding myself. I had attracted all this; the good, the bad and the ugly. Taking responsibility would help me to learn some very important lessons and move past the awkward moments into a future that I was choosing. It was vitally important for me to keep my focus with all areas of my life. When something drastic would happen in my personal world, I might take a few days to process all of it. I would be sure to give situations their due attention before getting back in full swing again. Focus: a necessary part of success that can simply not be ignored.

"It's not selfish-IT'S SELF CARE"

One of the very important lessons that I learned was self care. Many of us are taught from very early in life that we need to take care of everyone else. While a giving spirit is honorable, it is easy for us to get out of balance. Some people are truly self-centered and unloving but I am going to assume for the moment that you aren't like that. The people I am talking to today love to give to everyone else but seldom take time for themselves. If this is you, don't deny it to yourself. You stand a better chance of growing and moving forward by recognizing this weakness. While I am sure some of the people that you give to are thankful for the things that you do it is important to remember that you can't give from an empty cup. Do yourself and those who are important to you a favor; start taking time for yourself. Take time to meditate. Take time to take care of you. Without this personal care time you can easily lose focus.

For me, staying focused on family came naturally. My business is what could have easily been lost in the shuffle. Money may not be the most important thing that people want to focus on, but let's get real here for a moment. How much could I have changed my world or my children's lives if I remained a hostage to poverty? I didn't want to raise kids who felt that money was everything yet on the other hand I thought it was important for them to see that the more money you have, the more good you can do. Money is not evil; it's the love of money that is a vice. It's all about keeping your priorities straight. So I worked to keep focus on my business, knowing that it would be the core of several of the changes that I needed to make in life.

You want to know the secret?

I've been asked many times over the years what the secret to building my business was. When people ask me that as if I can give them a solid, life-altering three minute answer, it makes me laugh. Nevertheless, if you're looking for a little information to work with I can give you two key points that I believe are indispensable. The key to business building for me was passion and relationships.

Passion and relationship building are what it seems you can boil it down to. Think about it for a minute. Think about the volumes of career advice you've heard over the years. If you had a burning passion for what you do and you were focused on building meaningful relationships, wouldn't it be easy to find clarity in those "now what do I need to do" moments? You would be unstoppable. Years ago I hit a period where I was just stuck. I wasn't sure what to do next. I wasn't even sure what I wanted next. I had reached several goals and had not grown my vision beyond that point. One of my friends gave me the book "God Is a Salesman". It was this book that made me face the fact that I had lost my passion. Not only had I lost my passion but I had drifted off into this aimless pursuit of nothing! My days had returned to handling mundane tasks at hand and suddenly realizing that it was time to go to bed and watch some television before drifting off to sleep. Don't get me wrong; I was a busy person. At least that's what I had convinced myself. I don't know if you've noticed it or not but people can be very active, appear extremely busy, and yet accomplish very little. That was me. I wouldn't say that I was lazy. I had simply lost sight of my passion. Passion will propel you in the direction of your dream. Even if you aren't exactly sure how your dream is going to look at the finale. Passion will move you steadily in the right direction. It was definitely time to reignite my passion.

Then there's the matter of building relationships. I knew people. I had a huge contact list and I was actually staying in touch with them. But was I building relationships with them? No, I really wasn't giving them the time they needed. It's so true that "people don't care how much you know till they know how much you care". People don't really want to do business with a stranger. Heck, sometimes people don't want to do business period. But people are far more open to dealing with their friends. Chew on that for a minute. Imagine a knife salesman comes to your front door. Do you welcome him right in and thoroughly enjoy the presentation? Offer him a cup of coffee and give him a nice sized order before he leaves? I highly doubt it. In reality you're probably irritated that someone would show up unannounced and expect to take your time, even if just a few minutes. If you're anything like me you wouldn't even have to think about it; this poor guy simply is not going to get a sale out of you, right? Okay, now switch scenes. Now imagine one of your friends- a long time, close friend, got roped into hosting a kitchenware party. Do you need anything for your kitchen? Let's say you really don't this time. What do you do? You might explain to your friend that you really don't need anything right now. But chances are, you'll order a little something for yourself. Or you'll think of the wedding you have to go to or your sister's upcoming birthday and you'll find just the right gift that you can purchase through your friend; this way it will help her out as well. People are far more open to dealing with their friends!

At this point, I was still presenting business to people, but it was different. Not only was I lacking passion in my presentation (which is the equivalent of saying "I have this little...business...thing I do...but you probably wouldn't be interested, right?"), but I wasn't taking the time to build the friendship. I wasn't giving them a reason to trust me, to understand that I wouldn't steer them wrong just to put a buck in my pocket. Things weren't growing, and I was wondering why. I needed this reminder of the importance of relationship building.

That one simple gift from my friend held the reminder for me. Passion and relationships are the core of my business. It's people first, and the monetary success will follow along with all of the other blessings.

So where does our time together leave you? My hope is that you will remember that you truly do always have a choice. Fear will try to convince you otherwise. Just step beyond the fear. Know in your heart that "this too shall pass" and remind yourself often that you need to take care of yourself. Never feel guilty about taking care of yourself because in reality, you are benefitting everyone else in your life by doing so. Dig deep to find your passion- that which totally lights the fire within you- and follow that passion. Along the way build solid relationships with all that are meant to be a part of your process. Success might have many other components that are important but I know this – without passion and people, success will stay just out of reach for you.

I wish you all the best. May we all continue to grow, learn and prosper as we build relationships and love life.

Kim Rinaldi-Robey

Kim@theoilslady.com
www.theoilslady.com
www.kimrinaldi.vibrantscents.com
www.kimrinaldi.myningxia.com
www.youngliving.com/Kim

Kim Rinaldi-Robey resides in the Syracuse NY area where she is a wife and mother of three. Kim was raised in an entrepreneurial family and enjoys building business and empowering others to do the same. Despite being adamantly against Network Marketing, in August of 2000 she became passionate toward the use of essential oils and natural health. This passion propelled her into a successful career of sharing information and teaching others how to take control of their lives emotionally, physically, and financially with essential oils. This sharing has developed into a dynamic network marketing organization encompassing thousands of members in each of the United States and in over ten other countries.

Kim is a powerful advocate for change and a spectacular example of how making bold moves one can change their life dramatically. Her leadership skills have proven indispensable to her team. While teaching both personal growth and business skills she has proven exceptional in reaching her audience with warmth and passion. Being quick to connect on a heart to heart level she can motivate an individual or an organization to take the next right step.

Feel free to reach Kim at Kim@theoilslady.com . You can follow her blog at www.kimtheoilslady.com. She can also be reached through www.facebook.com/theoilslady, www.twitter.com/theoilslady or www.theoilslady.com

Chapter 7
Catalyst for Change

I come to you writing this chapter from a humble stand-point. I am simply a woman with a desire to connect with others and help them release the things that do not serve them in order to attain their hearts' desires and live their life to their ultimate benefit.

My life experiences have helped me to have a more insightful and compassionate understanding of others. I'm non-judgmental and truly believe that we all have a purpose in this life, and that is to live an abundant purpose-filled life full of joy.

Approximately four years ago I became friends with a woman named Lynne. As our relationship evolved from acquaintances to close friends, I did not initially realize the impact I was having on her life. As I continued on my personal journey of transformation and creating the life I always wanted, Lynne was watching my evolution and she was encouraged by the changes she was seeing. I asked her to share with me the ways in which I have impacted her and encouraged her self-development. She said the biggest way was by simply being a good friend to her and renewing her faith in friendship. Wow, that was a huge statement to me. When we met I had no idea that she didn't believe in friendship anymore.

Lynne's sister recently passed away and I was there by her side in a jiffy with a beautiful planter and card. I just sat with her and offered her a shoulder to cry on as she reminisced about the good times with her sister, and grieved from the loss.

A few months later she needed someone to take her for a medical exam and back home again. Lynne had no one; not even one of her two children offered to be with her through this ordeal. Again, I was there for her. I gave her a ride to the hospital and back home again. Because she did not have even her family to count on, this meant quite a lot to her.

Lynne shared that by watching me with my own family, plus working full-time in addition to all of the other activities I had undertaken (my spiritual studies and preparing to return to school) made her think about what she can do to become more fully vested in her own life.

Example is not the main thing in influencing others, it is the only thing.

~ Albert Schweitzer

Recently I noticed Lynne struggling with an ongoing situation in her own family. I could see that she was a bystander at her granddaughter's birthday party and I stepped right up to get her more involved. I took pictures of her and encouraged her to be more assertive in getting time with the kids when other family and extended family were basically just leaving her in the background.

At a later date, we discussed her confidence and assertiveness levels, and how she might improve on them. I fully understand her family situation and the estrangement from them. Despite that being the way it has always been and she's so used to it, she naturally doesn't want it to be that way. Lynne just did not have the courage or know-how to change the family dynamics.

Lynne told me that that was exactly what she needed to hear, and that she would try as much as possible to be there for her grandchildren, scooping them up in her arms and telling them "I'm your grandma and I love you!" without worrying about what the step-family had told them. Lynne is stepping up to the plate and not allowing them to walk all over her anymore! I'm so proud of her!!

"You cannot teach a man anything; you can only help him find it within himself."

~ Galileo Galilei

Lynne also knows my struggles and all I have given up in order to raise my own children and deal with all of the issues a family faces during and after divorce. She sees my growing strength and how I have risen above the adversity and challenges, not allowing myself to wallow in self-pity. Instead, she has seen me take control of situations and move forward, not letting anything stop me. Now she is doing the same thing by making necessary shifts in her own life in order to move forward, empowered with the knowledge everything will work out in divine time and be as it should with all of her needs being provided for.

Another individual who comes to mind is Paul whom I met on Facebook. Paul shared with me that through my words and posts on Facebook, and then through emails we exchanged, I have had a huge impact on his life. After reading my chapter from the book *Restoring Your Beautiful Life*, he found my ability to overcome such adversities remarkable and was truly inspired to let go of his own past and to deal with the guilt he carries for feeling he has somehow failed his children. He told me I have opened the door to other great authors and set the stage for his personal transformation, changing the course of his life to include his spirituality, eating healthier, and attending Tai Chi classes. Recently, Paul read his fortune cookie message to me. It read, "Our first love and last love is self-love."

"A lot of people have gone further than they thought they could because someone else thought they could."

~ Unknown

My purpose is to share my life experiences and insights in order to encourage others' self-development, pushing them to love and accept themselves for the beautiful and perfect person they are, and to learn how to reframe the way they see things. Each of us has issues in our lives. It is how we choose to cope with these issues that shapes our future.

I have learned self-love and responsibility through discovering and acknowledging what my real needs are, addressing my needs, and meeting them. I don't have to please everyone else or worry what others think about my thoughts, my feelings, or my ideas. You need to get to the place where you know yourself and understand what your needs are. We all are made perfectly and have gifts to share.

> "The greatest good you can do for another is not just to share your riches but to reveal to him his own."
>
> - Benjamin Disraeli

When I was asked to participate in this book the first question I pondered was "how have I made a difference?" People tell me I have impacted their lives, encouraged them, and given them the strength and confidence to make changes in their lives. But how have I accomplished this?

I give people an opportunity to see that it is possible to change your direction by re-arranging your focus and building on your attributes rather than letting life "happen". You can make lemonade out of lemons! You can change your focus to trying to better your own personal circumstances rather than living in your past.

I spent quite a bit of time thinking about how I have possibly assisted others in their personal growth and development. The best answer I could come up with is, simply by being my authentic self. I freely share my life experiences and insights through open communication, active listening, writing, and even Facebook. People see how I'm living and want to know how they too can overcome life's obstacles in order to experience more joy in their own lives.

By actively listening with an open heart, honoring others for who they are, and being my true self, I'm able to establish a relationship with others based on mutual respect. My goal is to help others recognize and come into alignment with their ideas, desires, and goals. When thinking negative thoughts you are out of alignment with your soul, or inner-self, which in turn creates a barrier between where you are now and the attainment of your heart's desire.

My personal transformation and self-development really got into full swing about 3 years ago when I met a man by the name of Jim Morningstar who is the founder of the School of Integrative Psychology I have been attending. This was the real catalyst for my personal development and spiritual growth. Jim introduced me to a wide variety of tools I continue to use and to share with others even today.

A key component to spiritual growth and development is the integration of the mind, body, and spirit in a cohesive connection. Through this you become balanced and whole. If one or more are neglected, you become unbalanced and your body will be in a state of dis-ease. I began a daily practice of meditation, walks, proper rest, eating healthier whole foods, and educating myself through reading and attending classes. I quickly noticed that I not only felt better physically, but I had a much better outlook on life.

No longer did I look at experiences as being good or bad. Instead I was appreciative for the lessons presented to me, and the opportunities for growth. While you may not realize it while in the midst of a situation, all of our experiences are opportunities for learning and growth.

Stop reiterating the negative scripts over and over in your head. These are statements such as, "I'm not good enough", "I don't make enough money", "Nobody could love me", and "I'm not smart enough". We all do this to ourselves at various times in our lives. We truly do become what we think about.

"Our minds have unbelievable power over our bodies."

~ Andre Maurois

What I learned is extremely powerful and has completely changed the way I live my life. You cannot be healthy and balanced if you are lacking in one or more areas. If one is unhealthy, they all will be off balance. Some of these tools are affirmations, meditation, and the connected breath, in addition to understanding our energy centers and cellular memory and the importance of practicing daily self-care, proper nutrition and exercise such as Tai Chi.

In February, I started attending the T'ai Chi Ch'uan Center of Milwaukee. T'ai Chi is form of martial arts and an excellent daily practice for relaxation, meditation, self-defense, and generally increasing your health. I continue to develop my understanding of this exercise and further integrate my mind, body, and spirit in order to create more balance in my life.

My connection, not only with Spirit but also with myself, has increased exponentially. I'm much more balanced and centered within myself. I feel more in tune with my purpose as I continue on the path towards living the life I have always wanted and am intended to live. Doors are opening as if a spiritual pathway is being cleared to assist me in reaching my goals. I sit quietly and tune into my own inner thoughts as I seek guidance in everything I do. My spirit of laughter and joy has come back into focus; I have found me again, and within that is my life's purpose.

Taking time to expand my knowledge, try new things, and explore my creativity have all been key components in my recent evolution. By walking outside of my comfort zone I became an author, attended a drum building class, and am now attending school to become a Professional Massage Therapist/Therapeutic Body Worker. Becoming a massage therapist is part of living my purpose and my desire to help others, especially those who are terminally ill or recovering from surgery or injury. There are actually people out there whose only source of physical touch is from massage. I find this to be very sad and disturbing- everyone needs human touch.

Change is always present for all of us, and reaching out to grow in new ways begets healthy improvements to our spiritual path to successful life. Everything that we are- our thoughts, feelings, and beliefs- are all an integral a part of living our purpose. You simply cannot live your life fully and on purpose if your mind, body, and spirit are not in sync. You will not be able to reach your full potential.

Yesterday I was clever, so I wanted to change the world.
Today I am wise, so I am changing myself.
~ Jalal ad-Din Rumi

I have completely transformed not only my daily activities, but also my thought process, or way of thinking as well, enabling me to live a more spirit filled life of purpose. I now devote every day to living my purpose. Some days are better than others, but that is part of the process of change. As I continue my journey down the spiritual path to life success, I realize that my purpose is to be me, and to be open to opportunities for growth and change.

What counts in life is not the mere fact that we have lived. It is what difference we have made to the lives of others that will determine the significance of the life we lead.
~ Nelson Mandela

Simplify your life and you will find greater peace. Clear the clutter from your life by letting go of the things you have been holding on to and no longer need. Don't make things complicated by holding on to every event in your life; this creates chaos and profoundly affects your life. We all have a tendency to hold on to old memories whether positive or negative and carry these around with us. Make a conscious choice to lessen the load you are carrying around in your backpack of life.

What happened in the past is just that- the past. If you cannot change these occurrences, events and circumstances, release them. This is never an easy thing to do, but it is a necessary step in healing your past experiences and moving into the life you have always dreamed of. It's time to lighten your load, to take out the trash you might say, and to tap into your creativity. Manifest your dreams and live on purpose.

Be realistic about what you do and do not have time for. This is all part of taking care of yourself and keeping the clutter down. When you take on more than you can handle it creates stress, which manifests chaos. Once you clear away the clutter, don't bring in more.

If you watch how nature deals with adversity, continually renewing itself, you can't help but learn.

~ Bernie Siegel, MD, Doctor, Author and Lecturer

By applying these techniques, I learned how to calm my mind and focus on the present moment. Through this process I also started realizing what it meant for me to live my purpose. This required transitioning of my thought process and way of living. I felt I was living my purpose by being a mother and focusing on taking care of others. While that may be partially true, some very important pieces were missing. Those pieces were practicing daily self-care, and learning how to stay in the present moment.

I would like to further share with you the changes I've made in my own life, and how they have helped me. I cannot emphasize enough the need to integrate your mind, body and spirit. Since they are all connected, you cannot neglect one and expect the others to be balanced. It's important to not only take care of the mental aspects, but also focus on the body. Stress depletes your body of essential nutrients and illness manifests from stress.

Making changes to my diet, taking vitamins, and getting more rest all helped to bring me back into better alignment and balance. I had chronic pain, was diagnosed hypothyroid, and discovered I had a severe vitamin D deficiency, which is unusual for a woman of my age. This is when I realized that I needed to change. I started taking vitamin supplements as well and making better choices with my foods. I began by avoiding processed foods whenever possible, selecting organic fresh fruits and vegetables, and cutting dairy out of my diet. I now eat much less meat, avoid fat and select gluten free items when possible. I also avoid white pasta or rice. Additionally, I have decreased my intake of caffeine.

These choices have changed my life for the better. I've noticed a huge increase in my energy level and I sleep better. I can definitely tell the difference by how I feel when I eat unhealthy food, forget to take my vitamins, or do not get enough rest. That really demonstrates to me the importance of what I put into my body and taking care of myself.

Learning how to stop living in fear and to cease running was another huge hurdle I had to overcome. I needed to let go of the past that I was carrying around and to get back to my truth; the truth of who I really am. It's been a long journey of self-discovery and reconnecting with myself, finding what is important to me, and what I want. I've always lived for everyone else.

> *"What we think determines what happens to us, so if we want to change our lives, we need to stretch our minds."*
>
> — Dr. Wayne Dyer

Human nature is to hold on to past hurts and mistakes. We allow ourselves to become defined by our story. Letting go and rewriting those old scripts is a very difficult thing to do! The first step toward change is to reframe the way you view the past. You can do this through reciting positive affirmations daily. Keep them on your mirror in the bathroom, on your nightstand, or make them your screensaver on your computer! Make it fun!

At first it's going to seem like it isn't working and you'll try to talk yourself out of it. By way of consistency and repeating to yourself that you are worthy, you are loved, you are deserving, you are beautiful, you are of value, you are provided for, and you are perfect just the way you are, your thoughts about yourself will begin to change dramatically. You will start to believe it, because it is true! I know you've heard it said "God doesn't make mistakes!" Well, He doesn't.

Standing in the mirror and looking into the eyes of your soul as you repeat these affirmations to yourself adds to the impact, and is very powerful. It's hard when you first begin this process. Like I said earlier, you may feel like they are just words and they don't have any meaning for you. It may be difficult to believe the words you're saying to yourself are true and to take ownership of the affirmations. After some time and sticking with it, you do begin reframing the way you look at yourself. You start to believe what you are saying. Everyone on this planet is worthy and beautiful in their own way.

You become what you think about

~ Earl Nightingale

We need to stop placing judgments on everything. Stop judging our emotions, our anger, our sadness, and our fears. Learn to let it be what it is, and appreciate each emotion. Acknowledge it and let it go; don't hold onto it.

I was used to not being heard and being told what I was thinking and /or feeling. Therefore, a lot of my past frustration came from not knowing how to amply express what I was feeling and get my point across in a manner that relayed my truth to the other person. I have learned how to appreciate my emotions and stay with them... to feel them. It's okay to be mad, sad, or glad- whatever you are feeling. Find healthy ways of expressing your emotions and the voice to express them while feeling safe.

Life doesn't need to be a struggle. It should be joyous and happy. It doesn't matter how much or how little you have in material things. What does matter is what you hold inside, and how you feel about yourself and the world you live in. Is it a safe place where all of your needs are provided for? Ironically, I find I'm happier with fewer material things. To me this equals less stress and less drama. I don't have a need to keep up with the Joneses. I would rather focus on what makes me happy, and helping others to achieve their happiness.

"When I hear somebody sigh, 'Life is hard,' I am always tempted to ask, 'Compared to what?'" "Life is a song – sing it. Life is a game – play it. Life is a challenge – meet it. Life is a dream – realize it. Life is a sacrifice – offer it. Life is love – enjoy it."

~ Sai Baba

Proper breathing and being "aware" of your breath is extremely important. Take full and complete breaths in order to get ample oxygen and increase your health. Also, pay attention to your body and the messages it's giving you. For example, let's say your throat is getting tight, your heart is beating fast, or you get a funny feeling in your stomach. These are all signals your body is trying to tell you something. When you're in the midst of some sort of negative situation you don't always pay attention to the warnings your body is giving you. You may feel the fear, but you are not addressing what the issue is. Neither are you doing what you really should do by getting out of that situation and moving on, or addressing the issue at hand.

Stop putting your energy and focus in the past and dwelling on the negative. Move forward and find gratitude in your heart. Live your life with appreciation, not guilt and regret. You will begin to notice a positive improvement in the way your view yourself and your life, and you will begin attracting the things you want in your life. The people that no longer serve your highest good will disappear from your life and you will attract healthier relationships. The power of positive thinking and the law of attraction are amazing! You can make a choice to focus on the positives and find gratitude in any situation. Pull on your strengths and care for yourself as you move forward creating your beautiful life.

You may have a fresh start any moment you choose, for this thing that we call 'failure' is not the falling down, but the staying down.

~ Mary Pickford

Good timber does not grow with ease; the stronger the wind, the stronger the trees.

~ J. Willard Marriott, Founder of Marriott Hotels

It hasn't been easy. There have been times when I've gone backwards. Nonetheless, I always keep moving forward. Like anyone else, I'm a work in progress. We are always evolving, learning, changing, and growing. We never stay the same. Now I find myself on a path of joy, abundance, and gratitude. Living in the know, truly knowing, who I am and what my purpose is. Believe in the beauty of you and your dreams.

The future belongs to those who believe in the beauty of their dreams.

~ Eleanor Roosevelt

Kimberly Pratte

Kimberly Pratte resides in Milwaukee, WI where she is a student at the School of Integrative Spiritual Psychology and Blue Sky School of Professional Massage & Therapeutic Bodywork. She is currently employed at an Executive Search firm as a Project Coordinator, and has co-authored three books.

Having recently opened a private practice, Kimberly's passion in life is to assist others along their journey of healing and self-discovery through sharing her own life experiences and the tools she has found to be beneficial in creating the life she has always dreamed of.

Kimberly S. Pratte
kimpratte@gmail.com
www.kimberlypratte.com

Chapter 8

It's Time to Get REAL!

It's a good thing that you are reading this book; it means you are ready to make positive and lifelong changes that will influence your lifestyle. Habits are chosen for a reason, and there are REAL issues that have gotten you to where you are right now. Trying to make changes without addressing the root of those issues will be futile. How do I know this? I have been there.

Hello, I am Lisa Schilling and I am a foodaholic and adrenaline junkie. I have a torrid past when it comes to eating and exercising; I dieted, binged, purged, took medication, exercised, burned-out, did nothing, and then the cycle continued. The good news is that I, and others like me, can experience recovery. Just like other addictions, where a substance or behavior is used to achieve a desired response, food addiction works much the same. My substance of choice just happens to be food, instead of drugs or alcohol. However, unlike other addictions, it is impossible to go cold turkey off food or the result is death. As you can understand, this does complicate the recovery process.

I embarked on a mission of health and fitness education, starting by acknowledging that my own health and fitness habits had declined and, in many areas, had become nonexistent. I felt that as a nurse, wellness coach, and former pageant winner, I knew better. In this, I discovered my first **Get REAL Point**: "Just because you know the right things to do does not mean you will choose to do them."

Thus my philosophy was born. We need to Get REAL! As my life changed and I became a mother and wife with a full-time job, I lost the ability to maintain my previously high self-care standards. Unfortunately, "experts" in this industry only tell people the highest standards that you would follow if you had all the time, motivation, and resources to work on achieving optimum health and balance. Many people start these programs and then give up due to how difficult they are to maintain.

It became clear that many people wanted to live healthier, but they needed something to motivate and keep them on track. I discovered a purpose- to get back what I once had, in the new lifestyle that I currently have. By helping myself, I would be able to help others who have found themselves in similar positions.

Magical Moderate Mentality

Starting small, at "less than" what *experts* said was optimal, made it easier to stick to my plan and actually see improvement. By refocusing your attentions and tying to link your actions to a deeper purpose, you can give traction to your inner motivation. Through thought shifting, reframing, and purposeful living, you have the ability to greatly improve your total wellness and increase personal balance.

Living a healthy lifestyle needs to become something you enjoy, look forward to, and live on a daily basis!

The Information Superhighway

The Internet, bookstores, and TV are full of information about what to do to achieve health and life balance, as well as how to do it. That is the problem- information overload! The amount of information can be so overwhelming that some people give up before they even start. To reestablish focus, develop meaningful attachments to your actions.

In addition, I have come to understand that the phrase "I don't have time" really means, "I just don't want to *that* badly." You will figure out a way to do the things you really want to do.

Change Your Mind, Change Your Body

Positive behavioral changes are made by creating meaningful thought-process changes in the mind. To improve your chances of successful behavior change, here are ten mental principles that can help you make healthy changes that last:

Tool #1 Making Healthy Changes that Last:

1. Identify your routine habits and what you get from them, the payoff.

2. Recognize any stress-based habits and what they attempt to neutralize.

3. Identify mental cues and triggers which encourage behavior choices.

4. Recognize your reward circuits, and what starts your reward cycle.

5. Identify and overcome any reward deficiencies.

6. Discover ways to reinforce desired behaviors. Create a new payoff.

7. Commit to training new habits and provide proper mental support for maintaining them.

8. Fully value your health and worth, and mentally reinforce this value daily.

9. Learn the role of neurotransmitters in the brain that affect behavior choice.

10. Begin to use brain chemistry to your advantage.

In order to enact this list, you must first understand more about habits. These are not only repeated physical behaviors; they can be repeated thoughts, emotions, or physiological responses.

Habit Havoc

Habits are learned and maintained through reward and reinforcement. Reinforcement associates the feeling of immediate well-being to whatever caused it. Rewards are anything that you perceive will increase your immediate well-being, whether in reality it will or not. They deal with your "perception" of an increase, not the increase itself.

Positive reinforcement creates reward and can produce immediate and long-term benefit. Anything that takes you from feeling just okay to feeling good creates a positive reinforcement. A behavior that is reinforced is more likely to be repeated, which is not always associated with a positive outcome.

Negative reinforcement creates "relief" from some perceived discomfort. It produces mainly immediate benefit but long-term harm, if repeated. Threat-based habits come from negative reinforcement, where you have gone from feeling bad, to now feeling neutral or less bad. The behavior is repeated not because it is necessarily a good choice, but as a way to avoid feelings that are perceived worse.

You create behavior change through repetition of the desired behavior. When you reinforce a behavior, it has the potential to become compulsive, which can then develop into addiction. Over time, brain chemistry can become altered to "need" the substance or behavior in order to achieve a perceived feeling of normalcy. Without the behavior or substance, withdrawal symptoms appear.

Basil Ganglia-The Mental Store House

Many addictions become mentally embedded within the brain, linked with cues and triggers, as the basil ganglia permanently stores habits and memories. These deep associations lie just under the surface waiting to be triggered. The constant triggering of those embedded links accounts for relapses and explains why addictions cause lifetime struggles.

Some compulsive habits have obvious triggers that begin the mental spiral of longing. This can create a "dependency cycle" where the trigger leads to the behavioral response, which then leads back to the trigger. This cycle is perpetuated when what people choose to use for relief, causes them further distress, e.g. overeating because of frustration with being overweight.

Dopamine-The Mental Reinforcer

People engage in potentially harmful behaviors for either reward or relief. Associations develop between cue and reward, which are then cemented in the basil ganglia (the mental storehouse for habits). This cue triggers the release of dopamine, a strong neurotransmitter, which provides a pleasant sensation or boost.

The more you think about and believe that the reward will be pleasurable, the greater the dopamine release. By altering your beliefs and expectations, you also alter dopamine release linked to past behaviors.

Compulsive over-avoidance is a relief-seeking behavior. It is a coping mechanism used to manage anxiety, depression, or fear, e.g. someone avoids healthy relationships because of a subconscious fear of having their heart broken.

Compulsions are common and often go unidentified. Uncovering and acknowledging your compulsions is the first step to taking control of negative behavior. The second step is to create a plan to circumvent it. The final step is implementing your plan in situations where you feel compelled to repeat the unwanted behavior.

Soft Addictions

The word "addiction" brings to mind things like alcohol and drugs. However, more subtle forms of addiction can sneak into your life and cause havoc because they are not often recognized. Judith Wright, author of *The Soft Addiction Solution*, explains, "Soft Addictions are those seemingly harmless habits like over-shopping, overeating, watching too much TV, endlessly surfing the internet, procrastinating—that actually keep us from the life we want. They cost us money, rob us of time, numb us from our feelings, mute our consciousness, and drain our energy."

Sneaky Time Stealers

While some screen time (TV, games or the internet) is fine, too much becomes a problem. Screen time can numb the mind, leading to more and more of your time spent in front of one. Count the costs; ensure that these seemingly harmless behaviors are not costing you more than they are providing. To discover and combat soft addictions you can use this six-step tool:

Tool #2 Combating Soft Addictions:

1. Recognize these behaviors: look for areas in your life where you might be using a behavior for the wrong reason; behaviors that are not adding value to your life.

2. Target each behavior specifically.

3. Discover the payoff you get from them.

4. Decide what emotion or feeling is attached to the behavior.

5. Examine more deeply, what the behavior is covering up. Ask yourself, "What am I avoiding by participating in this behavior? What is making me want to dull or heighten my emotions? What area of my life do I not want to confront? What root issue needs to addressed? What more could I get from my life if I limited or avoided this behavior?"

6. Replace the old behavior when you become aware of it.

Win the Mind Game

Many people struggle to adopt healthy habits like eating right, exercising, and stress management. Much of this resistance occurs in the mind.

Cravings are a strong subconscious desire for something, and are born in the hindbrain, the part of the brain that initiates desire for rewards. It reacts to a stimulus and that reaction forms a thought, which introduces that substance or activity to your mind. You can dwell on that thought and create a longing for it, or you can activate the conscious thinking part of your brain, and neutralize that thought.

Reward Cycle

The reward system will lock in a target behavior or substance, which triggers the brain to release dopamine. The longing for immediate gratification is so strong that it inhibits the prefrontal cortex, the thinking part of the brain, from being activated. The body will also release stress hormones to make the craving more compelling.

Purposely activating the prefrontal cortex will give you a fighting chance to make smarter choices when cravings strike.

Craving Reward

Cravings come from rewards that are reinforced. Anything that creates pleasure or a sense of reward can cause strong cravings because the brain learns to anticipate that reward. The more often you indulge that craving, the stronger your mental connection will become to it. Once you stop indulging your cravings, they will begin to decrease.

Reward Reinforcers

Feelings can be reinforced without your knowledge because they often occur on a subconscious level. You can combat further the cravings cycle, by attaching that behavior to the consequences instead of to the reward, thus rewiring how your subconscious will react to it. You can then begin to reprogram your mind to develop reward signals for behaviors you are trying to cultivate.

Think Smart

There are many things that you COULD do to lead a healthy balanced life. However, this abundance of choices can be overwhelming and often confusing. Under the pressure of multiple confusing options, people often choose not to choose.

Shift Your Thinking

Thought shifting or repatterning, works by taking an old negative way at looking something and reframing it in a more positive light. When you recognize negative thought patterns creeping in, you can stop them- and shift them. Recognize, Stop & Shift. This repatterning technique will give you a concrete way to uncover problem thought patterns and a way to replace them.

Tool #3 Seven Step Plan to Repattern Your Thinking:

To complete your repatterning plan, use a set of 3x5 cards. The goal is to create a portable system that you can regularly review and utilize.

Step 1. GOALS (G): Write out your positively stated goals, one goal per card.

Step 2. ACTION PLAN (AP): On the back of each card, create a practical action plan to implement each positive goal statements.

Step 3. ACCOUNTABILITY TASK (AT): Below each AP create accountability or ways to monitor and measure your progress. This provides the way you will measure progress, along with giving you a tangible consequence for not following your goal.

Step 4. ACCOUNTABILITY REWARD (AR): Below each AT create an incentive or reward for reaching your goal. This step provides positive goal reinforcement.

Step 5. NEGATIVE THOUGHT (NT): Use a new set of cards and write as many negative thoughts about each of the healthy behaviors you are targeting, one per card.

Step 6. POSITIVE AFFIRM (PA): On the back, rewrite that thought in a positive way (reframed). Be realistic and honest, not "I love to exercise," when you really do not.

Step 7. REVIEW (R): Review your cards daily. Stick to your accountability task and reward. For particularly tough tasks, write those reframed thoughts on post-it notes and put them where you will see them regularly, like the car dash or the bathroom mirror.

The Busyness Trap

Life is a constant balancing act. For each new commitment you take on, you must be able to devote the time and attention that it will take to maintain it. Trying to have it ALL creates an unhealthy & unrealistic schedule that can leave you feeling frustrated, overwhelmed and depressed.

Reality Check

Busyness has become an epidemic, stealing what is most important in life. Because of technology, you now have the ability to entertain, educate, or distract yourself at any time or place, with little to no physical effort.

This causes people to take on more than was ever intended and as a result, people are becoming mentally fatigued and physically sluggish. It becomes important to be selective in what you allow to fill your time. Set boundaries to protect your time and your best interests.

Developing Vision

In order to set boundaries, you must clearly identify your personal vision. Your vision may change dramatically as life changes, so this needs to be an ongoing process. Develop a distinct picture of "what matters most" to you; each person must discover their own internal vision for life.

Tool #4 Finding Internal Vision Exercise:

To help you develop your personal vision you may go to: www.getrealwellnesssolutions.com to download your free "FIVE x F.I.V.E. - Finding Internal Vision Exercise." This short worksheet asks five questions in each of these areas:

1. What is important to me?
2. What am I good at?
3. What happiness looks like to me?
4. What I know about myself?
5. What I need to change in my life?

This personal discovery tool allows you to determine your life direction, enabling you to accurately set "North" on your personal compass. From there you can easily create a personal vision statement based on what you have learned about yourself. The following is an example of a personal vision statement: *My purpose is:* to help others achieve personal wellness *by:* researching and creating tools to assist others in their journey, *using my talent(s) of:* writing and public speaking.

Seeking Alignment

Think about the things that the matter most to you in this world. You will experience true contentment when you align your behavior with those things. Anxiety, confusion, and discontentment are signals that you are not aligned with what matters most to you.

Cancel the Guilt Trip

Well-balanced people do not let what they *should have done* hold them back. Embrace that you are human and understand that everyone makes mistakes. This freedom allows you a fresh start each day and keeps your future from being limited by your past.

Living in Fast Forward

When you live with adrenaline surges from rushed behavior, downshifting to a normal pace can be a challenge. Adjustment starts when you recognize that the time pressures have been loosened. It takes time for that realization to sink into your subconscious mind. Taking time to be mindful and reflect on these changes can help to connect the conscious thoughts to the ones just beneath the surface.

Being constantly busy creates strong reinforced mental conditioning. The body adjusts to the demands put on it and can operate at full-capacity for some time. However, there is a limit to how long you can sustain that pace without creating damage.

Going Faster

When people feel short on time, they look for ways to speed up the things they already do. In time, you begin to forget how to go slower, and that is a high price to pay. A rushed life is superficial by necessity as you only allow enough time to skim the surface and this leaves no time for real connection with people or the things that bind people together and make life a meaningful experience.

Downshifting

Downshifting to a slower pace allows time for doing nothing, being with friends, daydreaming, and reflection. Find out where your thoughts would go if they were not challenged by the latest distraction. When was the last time you read an entire article, book, or even an email?

Tempo Giusto

Purposeful downshifting enables you to live a more fulfilling life in the midst of this fast-paced modern world. The speed you downshift into is an individual choice and unique to your special needs. This right speed or *tempo giusto*, as musicians would call it, requires finding what is important to you and ensuring you honor that in the way you use your time.

Acceleration Generation

The desire to have and do everything causes people to either accelerate their pace or squeeze in more than they can do and fully enjoy. Technology is an enabler and false friend to the acceleration generation. Living at an accelerated pace leads to less fulfillment in life. This causes further acceleration in an attempt to avoid confronting uncomfortable feelings. This fast life can feel good temporarily but like a drug, it soon wears off leaving you seeking more.

Breaking the Cycle

Many people find that it is the meaningful connections with people, places, and community, which bring about happiness. Slowing down is essential to make such connections.

Slowing down is like breaking any other habit- you must first make a connection with a real reason to slow down and deeply desire to do it. If you are worn out and run down, what do you have to lose?

Time Poverty

Many people report not having enough time to do all that they want to do. To combat this "time poverty" there are some people promoting a "slow movement," seeking to reconnect with life. Its goal is to create a cultural shift towards slowing down and experiencing the simple pleasures of life.

Reconnecting

Over time, people are conditioned into thinking that they need to be fast and to have what the fast life provides. However, deeper examination reveals that connectedness is more valuable than any material possession.

You can start by downsizing, reducing the amount of stuff that you have and must take care of. This can help to reduce excess responsibility, allowing for the enjoyment of what you still have.

Tool # 5 Setting Your Compass:

1. Divide a sheet of paper in half

2. At the top of the first column write SLOW.
   At the top of the second column write FAST.

3. Brainstorm all the benefits (PROs) of each.

4. Then draw a line under the pros and brainstorm all the negatives (CONs).

5. Carefully evaluate your lists.
6. Decide which direction brings you more peace and happiness.

7. Turn the paper over.

8. Brainstorm the behaviors that you want to move in this new direction.

9. Create a mission statement, defining the direction in which you want to move.

Time Sickness

The term "Time Sickness" was first coined in 1982 by American Physician Larry Dossey, who described it as the obsessive belief that "time is getting away, that there isn't enough of it, and that we must pedal faster and faster to keep up."

People are now able to do things more efficiently and quickly than ever before but instead of using the extra time created to enjoy life more fully, society pressures people to take on additional tasks to fill that space.

Techno-Excess Syndrome

Using technology and other timesaving devices is not harmful in and of itself; it is when overuse and dependence combine with inadequate downtime that there is real harm. Dr. Dossey concluded that a distinct pathology of stress-related illnesses, ranging from heart disease to nervous exhaustion, is being created by the beliefs fueling "time-sickness."

Physical symptoms will present when the mind or body becomes overburdened. Failure to make adjustments at this point can lead to more serious health deteriorations, and even death. Common signs are headaches, musculoskeletal pain, chronic anxiety, sleep disorders, autoimmune dysfunction, irritable bowel, and low-grade depression.

Time Anxiety

Not content to just relax and take a deep breath, people often check email, text, surf the web, or catch up on work, during any amount of "downtime," thus negating the concept and restorative benefit of "downtime. When caught in the spiral of time-anxiety, the purposeful insertion of a mindfulness behavior such as deep breathing, guided imagery, or progressive muscle relaxation can help to break the cycle.

Developing Mindful Awareness

Adding a daily regimen of quiet reflection and intentional awareness is essential to restoring health and time perception. Here are 10 ways to slow down and become more mindful.

Tool # 6 Being Mindful and Slowing Down:

1. Regularly evaluate your schedule for excess, purge where possible.
2. Guard unstructured time.
3. Focus on what is gained by going slower.
4. Seek to balance exertion and recovery time, both physically and mentally.
5. Set boundaries for technology usage.
6. Reduce excess stuff, simplify what you have, and must care for regularly.
7. Look for ways to connect meaningfully with others around you daily.
8. Purposefully savor each moment and task at hand.
9. Insert mindfulness behaviors into your routine.
10. Leave time daily for personal reflection.

Stability

Healthy habits need to be the norm, and not the exception. Many people who struggle with health related problems treat wellness behaviors as a task that they must complete to get over the hump. That is to say, they will do them in protest, and then they can return to living just as they are now. This lack of stability makes it an optional activity, not a routine part of your lifestyle.

Lasting Wellness

In order to achieve lasting wellness, there needs to be a shift in mindset, from sprint to marathon. Temporary plans can be easily influenced by how you feel, the weather or other external circumstances, but tasks associated with a deeper purpose become part of your regular routine and therefore are less subject to circumstantial changes.

Create time for exercise and nutrition on a regular schedule. Consider where you are now in your physical fitness, nutrition and stress management efforts, and then create a regular plan that builds slow and steady to a maintainable regimen.

The Tortoise and the Hare

Know where you want to be in your health and wellness status and start making small sustainable changes that will build life-long habits. Be cautious not to look so far ahead that you become overwhelmed.

The turtle power approach is slower but much more stable, and years from now, you will still be on the right path. The rabbit approach leaves you subject to circumstance and will have you starting and stopping again and again.

Create stable lifetime habits, not short-term diets, and you will finally find the wellness to enjoy the life you have.

Maintaining Long-Term Commitment

A friend of mine, Robert Wimer, coined the following terms: Trackers, Tweakers and Trekkers, and I loved the concept.

Trackers: If you simply show them what needs to be done and how to track their choices better, they can successful navigate change on their own.

Tweakers: With some basic guidance to tweak their current habits, this group will be able to adopt a more purposeful, consistent and healthful lifestyle. This group responds well to challenges, groups, and having accountability to keep them focused and on track.

Trekkers: This group has deeper needs, and plain guidance and tracking will not cut it. If you bounce from diet to diet or habit to habit with little to no success, struggle with your weight and making good choices, you are likely a trekker. Gaining personal clarity and clearly defining it can help trekkers uncover what has held them back and give them the tools to overcome what they find.

The Trek for Personal Wellness

The following steps will help you to discover your personal motivators and bring forth strategies that you can use in your trek for personal wellness.

Tool #7 Creating a Personal Wellness Strategy

1. Set your *attitude* concerning health, balance, and purpose. Define your intention, visualize your desired identity, and write down your goals.

2. Write out a list of "What Matters Most" to you and be specific. Use this list to create a personal vision statement.

3. Commit to spend your time in a way that reflects what is important to you. Regularly evaluate your schedule to ensure that you stay in alignment with what matters most to you.

4. Commit to value and protect your personal time. Say no to extra obligations.

5. Know your goal! Be clear WHY it is important to you to reach your goals.

6. Make a commitment to *consistent moderation* in the areas of food intake, activity, and personal relaxation time.

7. Ensure that your thinking supports your goals and moves you closer to your personal vision, not away from it.

8. Stop negative thoughts when you become aware of them and then shift those thoughts into a positive frame.

9. Be mindful of your internal dialogue. Write down common reframed thoughts and post them where you can see them regularly.

10. Regularly review your written, goals, vision, and plan to achieve it.

Aligning with What Matters Most

When you honor your inner spirit, you will always be able to give, do, and be more. There are only so many hours in the day, and trying to add more things without taking something away becomes a burnout issue.

Whatever your issue is, keeping a detailed calendar or time journal can uncover it. You can use this information to create changes, allowing you to solve problem issues. Also, be sure to allow a nonnegotiable time buffer between each activity. This "margin" gives you room to move things around and to breathe. Margin needs to be purposefully built into your schedule.

Time for Pruning

No time for you? Then you need to prune from your schedule the activities that no longer bear fruit or reward you. Begin this personal evaluation by creating a "What Matters Most" list. If an activity does not line up with your list, look for ways to remove it. As your schedule opens up, you may begin to add personal improvement activities that recharge your batteries.

Tool #8 Creating What Matters Most List:

1._____

2._____

3._____

Boundaries

Like a traditional fence, boundaries keep out what you do not want in your space, and keep safe what you do want in your space. Creating personal boundaries is important when people make demands on your time. You need to have clear guidelines to measure against when deciding how to spend your time based on your "What Matters Most" list and personal values.

Balance and Align

"Time blocks" allow you to clarify your focus, creating awareness over what you allow to fill your time. People often struggle through their day, out of the flow of alignment.

Staying aligned and balanced will affect how you feel, as well as the choices you make. Learning to balance your routine is essential to staying well.

Time Block Scheduling

Your Time Block Schedule is a personal outline that shapes how you choose to move through your day. It creates flow, by establishing a guideline based on what you need to accomplish and what is important to you.

Tool #9 Time Blocking Your Schedule:

1. Determine the main areas that you need to make time for in your day.

2. Further define what is included in each area as sub-headings using the outline form.

3. Take the sub-headings and list under them (in Bullet Points), appropriate tasks for that time.

4. Now begin to allot an amount of time to spend on each Heading. During the time allotted for each Heading, you can work on any of those Sub-Headings or Bullets.

5. Allot time for things that commonly "steal time" from you (distracters) e.g. emailing, texting, phone calls, social media etc.

Using Your Schedule

Focus only on what you have allotted for that time block and avoid becoming distracted by things you have blocked for other times in your day. For an example of a Time Block Schedule, you can visit: www.getrealwellnesssolutions.com.

Have Your Cake

It has been said that, *"You can never have it all"*- at least, not all at the same time. Having a hectic and overwhelming schedule leads to unfocused thinking; at work, you are thinking of the things that need to be done at home, and vice versa. In an attempt to keep all the plates spinning, something always gets dropped. There comes a point where you have to "Get REAL!" You can only do so much.

Triple A Approach

One way to develop clarity is by using the Triple A Approach, Acknowledge, Accept and Act, as a way to define and refine the issue.

Tool #10 Using the Triple A Approach:

1. **Acknowledge** what is really happening e.g., I Acknowledge that I use busyness as an excuse to not exercise.

2. Decide what you are willing to **Accept** about it e.g., I am willing to Accept that although I am busy, I can make, and do make, time for the things that are important to me.

3. Create a plan to **Act** in a more purposeful way e.g., I will plan to Act, by scheduling exercise as an appointment and linking it to the outcome I desire.

Overwhelm and Dread

Most people have a full to-do list, and it is possible to become so overwhelmed that you feel defeated before you even start. For many, dread leads to procrastination. When you catch yourself saying **I can't, I'm not, or I don't,** consider that you might be getting ready to place a *false* limit on yourself. False limits are lies that people tell themselves, in order to avoid dealing with uncomfortable feelings or difficult circumstances.

Taking Ownership of Life

The lies that people tell themselves actually limit them from what they are capable of doing or being. To overcome this common problem, take on the situation by using the Triple A Approach. This approach gives you ownership of an issue, by providing a proactive *plan*.

Life-Balance Tool Box

The 10 life-balance tools offered here are for self-discovery and goal setting. Designed to help you to discover more about yourself, so that you can make aligned choices that move you closer to the happiness you seek. Keep these tools tucked in your personal toolbox and be sure to use them *before* you have an emergency. Remember, life is about your journey, not reaching a destination; so choose to enjoy the ride.

LISA SCHILLING RN, BSN, CPT

"Your Guide to Wellness, Through Personal Alignment"

Lisa is a Registered Nurse, NSA speaker, author/writer & recovering pageant queen, who spreads *hope* with her Get REAL approach to wellness. She guides & inspires people to create a wellness plan, which aligns them with a deeper purpose, allowing them to live their *best* life, see their *true* beauty, & embrace their REAL value.

Lisa is passionate about spreading this message of *hope* and *acceptance* to help others be PROactive about their wellness and not simply REactive. Using her knowledge and enthusiasm, she inspires people to value and appreciate who they are, on the way to where they want to be.

Today society moves so fast! Busyness and distraction drive people to do more and more and enjoy it less and less. Lisa knows first-hand the pressures to be thin, attractive and to do it all. Going from a former pageant queen to a working wife and mother of three active boys, Lisa illustrates how life is full of change.

Through her own journey of self-criticism and guilt, she emerged with a new philosophy...It is time to Get REAL! Lisa teaches from the powerful life lessons she learned through struggling with weight and body image issues. Now a sought after speaker, Lisa's humorous, and refreshing point of view resonates with audiences and sparks their internal motivation.

Lisa is the author of "The Get REAL Guide to Health & Fitness-FIVE STEPS to Create Your Own Personal Wellness Plan." She is also the creator of the "Get REAL A.C.E.S." chair exercise DVD series and writes a weekly newspaper column "Wellness Matters," which is broadcast on the radio as a PSA. She has over 100 expert articles published in ezinearticles.com where she is a Diamond Author. Lisa is also an expert contributor to Cardiologix magazine.

Lisa's fitness credentials continue to grow. She is a Certified Personal Trainer, Certified Group Exercise Leader, Practical Yoga Instructor, AFAA Biggest Loser Pro Trainer, and she is a Certified Instructor for "Live Like Your Life Depends On It," a managing chronic disease group program, as well as the "Arthritis Foundation Exercise Program."

Lisa has been featured nationally on the Lifetime network's "The Balancing Act." She has developed two full-day wellness seminars that she travels to share with audiences across the country. ("Wellness Matters" and "Worship & Wellness") For more information, or to book Lisa to speak for your group, visit her website, www.getrealwellnesssolutions.com. While you're there claim your FREE Bonus Gifts, & sign up to Get REAL Access to a treasure trove of FREE Gifts designed to help you bring REAL wellness solutions into your life.

ENDORSEMENTS FOR ROBYN PODBOY

"When was the last time you listened to your inner wisdom? In her chapter, Life is not about finding yourself, it's about creating yourself, Robyn Podboy gives us four simple ways to do just that; reconnect with our innate creative resources. Her words are filled with rich nuggets of wisdom. She offers effortless and clear 'doorways' that lead us to the treasured voice of truth within us."

- Dena DeLuco NLP
  Success Coach, Hypnotherapist
  Co-Author, *Step into Your Best Life*
  www.MindDeva.com
  "Celebrating a woman's prerogative to change her mind"

"It has been my honor to have attended many of Robyn's dynamic and empowering workshops. I am so grateful for her innovative and artistic talents! Her unique and thoughtful way of teaching has completely transformed the way I write and create my life!"

- Jaci Clark
  Principal Art Director and Founder of Jaci Clark Photography
  www.jaciclark.com

Chapter 9
Re-create Your Life

Life is not about finding yourself it's about creating yourself.

Using creative methods to quiet the mind and go into the heart for the expansion of expression has brought a healing joy to my life and to the lives of others who have done this kind of work. Dive into your creative divinity. The center for unconditional love is located in the middle of your chest. This is the fourth chakra which governs the heart, and is where your creative powerful energy is always available. Turn your attention to it, LISTEN; trust your inner wisdom.

Children naturally tune into their inner knowing. Somewhere between jumping rope, playing catch, signing songs, paying mortgages fear of job loss and health issues our vibration shifts; our inner voice is silenced.

Science is now proving that technology (cell phones, computers, etc.) And even the food we eat can contribute to the shift in our vibration.

When was the last time you heard your inner voice? Has it been so long that you don't remember?

As I reflect back I do remember; each week Mom would return from shopping with a new coloring book for me. I just loved to color each and every page. The smell of new crayons was heaven to me. This was an area where I felt most connected to myself! It became a meditation for a six year old. I was bringing each page to life with beautiful colors while getting lost in the picture that I was creating. My thoughts slowed; my mind drifted into peaceful tranquility my inner voice was speaking and I listened.

When you are creating (whatever you may be creating) do you feel more like yourself? In the creative space (heart space) we are connected to self and simultaneously connected to source. We are open to receive all that is. The potential is unlimited.

As a young person when I needed that quiet time, I could be found coloring, drawing, or rearranging furniture, without being aware of it I was creating my life's purpose. The joy of my professional career is in teaching the creative methods that have worked for me. Each tool I have developed has helped me go within to listen to my intuition. The answers to my questions are within me. I could hear what my heart was telling me. Like Dorothy in the Wizard of Oz I have everything I'll ever need right in my own back yard. This is true for us all. "There's no place like home."

There are many creative methods for going within to listen. Here are my favorite techniques that have helped me hear my inner voice. They are simple, fun and you can use them anytime you need to stop, listen, and hear your inner voice.

Write to Shine® *Trust Your Knowing Heart*

"For years I thought it necessary to go up and out for answers or find them in someone else's perception. I now know the truth of self is found within."

One of my favorite tools as a method to find my hidden voice to listen to my heart is creative writing. A wonderful writer, Kathleen O'Dwyer, turned me on to this kind of creative connection.

Each class or private mentoring session is designed to get you out of your head (chatter) and drop into your heart space (real) so you can hear your heart whispering to you. A lead-in question ignites your mind to respond. The key to this exercise is to keep writing for the allotted time. Don't stop to "think" about it; just write! The shift can feel as though your crown has opened up and a warm white light follows straight down to open your heart.

The first few minutes your page maybe full of gibberish or doubt and that's ok it's part of the process. Just write down what you are feeling. Your truth will be writing. You may find yourself amazed at what you have written; as if someone else has put the words on the paper. "Did I write that? Yes I did!" This is extremely therapeutic, sometimes emotional. Your imagination comes alive. By moving your focus from your head (losing your mind) to your heart (divine truth) you are amplifying your inner voice to be heard.

At the start of one workshop I asked each participant to write a single word on a piece of paper, fold it, and then place it in a bowl to be used later. When the time came I had everyone think of that one nagging question they couldn't seem to answer. After writing the question on the top of their page, the bowl was passed, each one randomly selected a folded paper. As they began the exercise the answer would be revealed in the paper they had chosen.

One of the participants, Jaci wrote the question, "What do I do about Robin?" They had a long standing friendship which now seemed to be at an impasse. Robin had betrayed their friendship by lying and keeping secrets from her. Jaci opened her answer to find the word "Help" on the paper. As she began to write something magical happened. Jaci realized that her own inner dialog was her connection to the divine (her inner knowing). She had it all along! The word "help" in her writing lead her to another question "Could I see myself continuing this friendship?" The more she wrote the clearer the answer had become. All she needed to do was ask the question, get out of her head and write from her heart! Amazing!

During this same exercise another person, Angie, expressed disbelief that this one word would be the answer, "It has nothing to do with anything" she exclaimed "*Giraffe* are you kidding me." With my instruction she kept writing. After the exercise I asked if anyone would like to share. Of course Angie was the first one to volunteer. Her question was "Why can't I see myself like others do?" As Angie shared her writing you could hear the shift go from her head (lots of chatter) to her heart (truth) seeing that she was elegant and magnificent. Angie shared many characteristics of the graceful giraffe! She was overwhelmed and excited with her discovery.

Other participants also shared that they found inner wisdom and clarity through this method. They are listening and discovering their own power to transform themselves. Using this method as a daily practice brings you to a place of silence and gives you an opportunity to listen.

Each time you use this exercise it becomes easier to quiet your mind and get into your heart space to have that inner dialog with your higher self like Jaci discovered. Place your hand on your heart and ask. "What is it that I need to know?" You will be able to hear what it has been whispering to you.

Understand what cannot be understood, hear from the heart~ Rumi

Does Anyone Remember Laughter?~Robert Plant

Laughter has always been such a big part of my life that I started to research the healing benefits for your mind, body and spirit. I know that whenever I am laughing I am indeed closer to Source. Have you ever walked into a place where there is laughter? You wonder why people are laughing. You look over to see what is so funny, you can't help but smile. You might say to yourself, "I want to laugh like that". Who doesn't like to laugh? Who doesn't like the way laughing makes you feel? Laughter is a method to lift you from a lower vibration to a higher one. And even better, you can fake it. Your *body* doesn't know the difference. Nothing works faster or more consistently to bring your mind, body and spirit back into balance! It costs nothing to laugh.

When I was 7 years old my grandparents took me to see *Mary Poppins*. Mary was an English Nanny who comes to take care of two children whose parents are too busy with their own lives to care for the basic needs of their children. In my favorite scene there is an emergency at Mary's Uncle Albert's house. When they arrive they find Uncle Albert laughing so hard that he is floating up to the ceiling and can't come down! He can't stop laughing! Soon they are all floating up on the ceiling with Uncle Albert laughing together, enjoying that amazing infectious feeling. This can be seen as a metaphor for the way laughter can "lighten" a mood. Laughter gives you a "floating feeling".

Here is what Melinda Smith, MA., Gina Kemp, MA., and Jeanne Segal, Ph.D., say the effects of humor and laughter do for the mind, body and spirit.

Laughter brings about an emotional high which can help you see problems from a different perspective, (an Uncle Albert point of view) especially those of a stressful nature. When you choose to find humor in challenging circumstances, you shift your emotions.

Adds Joy and Enthusiasm to Life ~ Happiness is contagious. Just hearing laughter primes your brain and readies you to smile and join in the fun. Humor is a powerful and effective way to heal resentments, disagreements, and hurts. Laughter unites people during difficult times.

- ~ Reduces Anxiety and Fear ~ Humor shifts perception, allowing you to see situations in a more realistic, less threatening light. A humorous outlook on life creates psychological distance, which can help you avoid feeling overwhelmed.

- Relieves Stress ~ Laughter helps you relax and recharge. It reduces stress and increases energy, enabling you to stay focused.

- Improves Attitude ~ Enhances amusement, dissolves distressing emotions. You can't feel anxious, angry, or sad when you're laughing.

It is well known fact that a "good laugh" does the "body good." It's true. Your body physically changes! Every time you laugh, you exercise seventeen different muscles in your face. People can see it. You can feel it. You Shine. This is your appearance in it's truest form. You look good!!

While inside your body, laughter produces natural opiates. It increases oxygen levels, which releases endorphins in your body (the hormones which make you happy).Laughter reduces cortisol (that's the stress hormone that contributes to belly fat). You can get a certain "floating like" feeling from it. Just like Uncle Albert, you just can't help it.You'll find yourself sleeping better and feeling healthier. Laughter slows down the rate of aging, stops depression, strengthens the immune system, and lowers blood pressure. Laughter just may help protect you against a heart attack. One good belly laugh is the same as "internal jogging." Now that is my kind of exercise!

- Lowers Stress Hormones ~ Boosts immunity, decreases stress hormones and increases immune cells. It will help infection-fighting antibodies, thus improving your resistance to disease.

- Decreases Pain ~ Laughter triggers the release of endorphins, the body's natural feel-good chemicals. Endorphins promote an overall sense of well-being and can even temporarily relieve pain.

- Relaxes Your Whole Body~ a good, hearty laugh relieves physical tension and stress, leaving your muscles relaxed for up to 45 minutes.

- Prevents Heart Disease~ Laughter protects the heart. Laughter improves the function of blood vessels and increases blood flow, which can help protect you against a heart attack and other cardiovascular problems.

Yes it does a body good! The benefits are endless.

Author, Rev. Michael Beckwith from the book (and movie) *The Secret, The Laws of Attraction* says, "Laughter heals your spirit, and this is when you are connected to your soul!" You are glowing from within like a lighting bug. This is your light.

- Strengthens relationships ~ Humor and playful communication strengthen our relationships by triggering positive feelings and fostering emotional connection. When we laugh with one another, a positive bond is formed. This bond acts as a strong buffer against stress, misunderstandings, and frustration.

- Attracts others to us~ Laughing with others is more powerful than laughing alone. Laughter is contagious. Shared laughter is one of the most effective tools for keeping relationships fresh and exciting. Being playful also adds joy, vitality, and resilience to all of your relationships.

~ Enhances Teamwork ~ Helps soothe conflict, promotes group bonding. Humor is infectious. When shared, it binds people together and increases happiness and relationships in the workplace.

Tap into your own "power" of happiness. This can begin with a smile.

When I was in my early thirties, my closest and oldest childhood friend was diagnosed with leukemia. We were so young disease and death were strangers to us. She was living in Chicago while I lived in Florida at the time, so we were limited to phone calls. We found ourselves laughing (although terrified of what was happening).We laughed at everything from Miss Ratchet the nurse, to the dozens of blood transfusion she was receiving. With each one, we would imagine who the donor was and then make up a story of how she would inherit each of their personalities. The laughter was loud on both ends of the phone! We shifted through by using laughter to help us both move beyond our fear. Sometimes she wasn't sure if she was high on all the drugs they were pumping into her, or the awesome humor we shared. I think laughter helped her survive; laughter indeed is the best medicine.

Laughter is the best addiction I have found! I love it so much that I became a Laughter Yoga Instructor. Finding a Laughing Yoga class helps you when you are having trouble lifting into laughter. It was founded by Dr. MadanKataria, MD, and his wife Madhuri Kataria.

This class will teach you methods for a shift and you will feel the benefits immediately! Laughter Yoga sessions start with gentle warm-up which include stretching, clapping and body movements. This helps remove self-consciousness to develop feelings of innocent playfulness. Be a kid again! Breathing exercises are used to warm up our lungs for laughter, followed by a series of 'laughter exercises'. The exercises open up your imagination which will then lead to sincere unconditional laughter.

I have found in the classes I facilitate that at first you *will* fake it; you may even feel a little silly. But keep with it because all of a sudden the real laughter will surface and become genuine. By the end of the class you have lifted your vibration and you feel exuberant. The light stretching, clapping and breath work are the yoga part of the class. The motto is "no pain no pain" so; just do what is comfortable for you. It's the perfect exercise for people in nursing homes or hospitals; for people who have difficulty standing. Laughing Yoga can all be done sitting down if you prefer.People leave with a feeling of rejuvenation and pure joy. Some actually can feel their core muscles for the first time in years! Laughter Yoga is innocent, fun, and great exercise for the soul.

How do you bring more happiness and laughter into your life? Try some of these simple tools to keep on hand in case you need a lift

~ Smile ~Try smiling at everyone you meet and see the results. Smiling is the activation of laughter. This is contagious.

- Be grateful ~Consider all the good things in your life. Keep a gratitude journal. This will separate you from negative thoughts.

- Seek out people who routinely find the humor in everyday events. Their playful point of view and laughter are attractive.

- Be spontaneous ~Release inhibitions, and the fear of being judged.

- Lighten Up ~Take yourself less seriously. Just Laugh.

- Be a child ~ Pay attention to children. They are the experts on playing, taking life lightly and laughing. Don't be afraid to be silly or goofy.

- Remind yourself ~ This is funny or where is the humor in this?

Your sense of humor is one of the most powerful tools you have to make certain that your daily mood and emotional state support good health.
~Paul E McGhee

In art the hand can never execute anything higher than the heart can inspire
~Ralph Waldo Emerson

While researching material for my "Write to Shine" workshops, I stumbled across an amazing healing technique called Touch Drawing, founded by Deborah Koff-Chapin, director of The Center for Touch Drawing. Touch Drawing is a simple yet reflective way of drawing with your fingertips; kind of like finger painting without the mess. I found myself eager to try this tool to connect with my inner self. I discovered it to be a beautiful healing art form and transformational tool. It's another way to journey inward. I love it!

It is easy all you do is roll artist's paint on a smooth board, place lightweight tissue paper over the paint and touch the paper with your fingers. An imprint is made on the back side of the paper. You create from your heart space trust your intuition, knowing that your manifestations come straight from the heart and the flow comes through the hands. Once you have finished the drawing, turn the paper over and see the work of art. Once again you may surprise yourself with what your heart and soul are whispering to you.

This is marvelous expressive method inspires desire which will flow freely from your heart. You will let go of any judgment and negativity from your inner ego. By using this method of creativity, you will see anew perception that has been awakened by your soul. What is so magnificent is that you don't need any artistic experience or dexterity. Your soul is the artist.

Many times you will be able to see different images surface as the paint becomes fully dry. In the classes I have facilitated a wonderful self-expression comes alive with each new drawing. The participants start out a little like they do in the "Write to Shine" class; coming from their head, but, after the first couple of drawings the flow comes deep within their heart and soul.

When you set out to use this method of connecting to Self, you will find that the materials are as easy to have readily available as a journal and a pen. To enhance your experience, go outside draw in nature. Listen to many different types of music to see how different emotions your drawings will reveal. In one class "the artists" listen to music while closing their eyes to go deep inward. Each drawing uncovered a hidden meaning. Another wonderful experience is to have the consistent sound of beating drums; this can bring to the surface many manifestations of self- you will be fascinated.

Most of all have fun with it. This is your time to be one with yourself and Source. A time for creative energy. This method is so wonderful that it can be used for everyone. Anyone can do it! Create a bond in a group by sharing your drawings (or not) interpreting what they mean to you. Use your imagination to create the perfect environment for your experience.

This method is used in many different areas in the healthcare industry. Many of the "artists" are people that are recovering from a stroke, serious illness or in hospice. They find the joy of a soul expression once again for some, it's the very first time. Children attending the workshops explore their imagination while drawing their wishes on the paper. "It's very fun"and allows them to express many feelings.

When you do things from your soul, you feel a river moving in you, a joy.
~ Rumi

<u>Listen to the music of you heart</u>

Music is another way of listening to your inner voice. The vibration of music of course can be heard, but the feeling that stirs inside of us invigorates the soul. I haven't met one person that doesn't like music! I know there are different types of music that we may not care for but we are all individuals and different notes stir different emotions in all of us. A friend of mine, Rick DiClemente (an Intuitive Astrologer), said something to me that I immediately resonated with. He said that at the precise time you were born, the universe struck a beautiful chord that is your unique vibration; you are an important part of this magnificent universal symphony!

What I love about music is that it transports me deep within myself when I'm meditating, bringing me clarity. I hear my inner voice. Music supports me to become inspired (in-Spirit) with my creativity. Whatever I am working on, whether it is myself, creating workshops or painting the living room ceiling, with music, I am connected and open to receive. Opening my heart space with music brings back memories of the past and it brings the joy of the future. Music has all the healing benefits that laughing does for the mind, body and spirit.People can maintain a healthy life by listening to music.

I also love the music of nature. There is nothing better than being at the beach hearing the sounds of the waves washing up on the shore, the way trees sing in the wind or rain falling from the sky even the quietness of the snow.

I recently took a workshop on the healing effects of singing bowls and the sound vibrations that resonated with me were astounding. It seemed to bring me to the music of my soul. I felt as if I was one with the music and I was part of the universal symphony! I felt this openness and wholeness with everyone who was in the workshop with me. Through the music, we were one. My children tell me this is the same emotion they feel when they return from a Radiohead concert!

The music is all around us, all you've got to do is listen
~August Rush

You had the power all along my dear
~ Glenda the good witch

These amazing methods of listening to our inner voice and opening up the possibilities that are endless have been life changing for me. As we continue to grow and share, I invite you to try them out; find the tools you can use. Your inner voice may be heard whenever you are being creative. That can be what you choose it to be. Whether it be gardening, cooking, photography or painting your toenails, just slow down and LISTEN; "Choose this moment to do what brings you joy with the peace and knowledge that you can make a different choice at any time!" We are all given everything we will ever need inside of ourselves. Shhhhh… what is your heart telling you?

Spirit is always calling you forward. Trust this truth and listen to your heart.
You are always divinely guided. Pay attention, be present, and allow your divine guidance to show you the yellow brick road to your dreams.
~ Sierra Goodman

Robyn Podboy

Robyn Podboy is the Owner of "Shine Your Light Now" She is a Personal Growth Facilitator, Published Author, Inspirational Speaker, Heal Your Life® licensed workshop leader, Laughing Yoga instructor, Touch Paint Facilitator. Robyn creates and facilities empowering, fun workshops and retreats to unlock your authenticity for personal growth. Robyn lives her life through the eyes of optimism and humor, helping others "Shine in their own light." She grew up in the northern suburbs of Chicago Illinois and now resides in Ohio with her husband and two sons.

robynpodboy@aol.com
www.shineyourlightnow.com

Dedicated:
To Bella Nitesh

Acknowledgements:

With much Love and Gratitude to my amazing husband, Tony, for your steadfast support, loving friendship, and gentle guidance. To my sons, Alex and Nate for encouraging me to share the discoveries of my journey with others. To my friends, Dena DeLuco, Jaci Clark and Deana Tareshawty, for their inspiration, love and friendship. I am especially grateful to my mom, Fran Blaesing for your unwavering love, support, and for always encouraging me to listen to my heart!

Endorsement

Sabrina Peterson offers fresh insights about health, weight control and looking better. So what's new? Imagine a gallon of milk sitting right there. Now imagine 10 gallons. That's how much weight Sabrina lost and kept off and now you can find out what she did to make it happen!

- Kevin Hogan, PsyD, Author of The Science of Influence

Chapter 10
The Doctor of the Future is You

"The doctor of the future will give no medicine, but will interest his patients in the care of the human frame, in a proper diet, and in the cause and prevention of disease."
– Thomas Edison

When it comes to your health, the future is now. There is no time like the present. You should ask yourself, "What am I doing right now that is harming or helping my health?"

Attaining better health requires three basic things:
- Diet
- Exercise
- Commitment

What did you have for breakfast this morning? What kind of coffee, tea or other beverage are you having? If it's lunch or dinner time, what's on your plate? How much plain water have you had to drink today? How many vegetables, fruits, whole grains or servings of lean protein and dairy have you eaten? Did you work out or do you have an appointment with yourself to get some exercise today, or at least three times this week?

In this digital age, we have unlimited access to a never-ending stream of television shows, infomercials, online ads, magazine and news articles all touting the newest, fastest and best ways to 'get healthier', 'lose weight', 'achieve six pack abs' or the 'perfect legs, butt, arms, etc'. Most of that information is contradictory. No wonder the US, with a 33% obesity rate, is the fattest nation in the world.

Choices = Results

"Real change happens, when the pain of staying the same is greater than the pain of changing."

-Sheldon Kopp

Oprah's trainer Bob Greene asks people three very insightful questions when helping them set goals for weight loss and fitness:

1. Why are you overweight?
2. Why do you want to lose weight?
3. Why haven't your past attempts at weight loss been successful?

I don't want to imply any assumptions with the above questions but there's a good chance that if you're reading this you could be overweight, obese, needing to lose a few pounds or even a 'skinny fat' person. Statistics say that at any given time, approximately 45% of Americans are on some type of diet and we spend $1-2 billion dollars every year on fitness and weight loss programs.

Having worked with hundreds of people in the past 10 years, I know that we are all smart enough to know what we should do in order to live healthier lives. Just because we "know" doesn't mean we choose to "do". Everything is a choice. Every decision you have made up to this point has gotten you where you are right this moment, and that applies to all areas of your life.

I don't want to put too much emphasis on weight or weight loss. There are healthy people of all shapes and sizes in this world. To assume that only people who are a certain weight according to their height are "healthy" is, in my opinion, an antiquated system of measuring health and fitness. I also want you to forget about caring too much about your Body Mass Index (BMI) because in my experience, that number is just far too general. Instead, if your body fat percentage is in a healthy range and you score average to good on a few basic fitness tests, I would say you are healthy no matter the number on the scale or the size of your pants.

More than anything, I want you to let go of the things that aren't helping you move forward toward better health, especially a lack of faith in your ability to do so. Becoming healthier really isn't that hard. As I tell my clients all the time, "Don't make it any harder than it needs to be." There are simple things you can do that will, over time, make big impacts on your health if you will just do them consistently.

Don't "Just Do It", do it consistently!

Back in November 2001, I weighed 291 lbs. and wore size 26 clothes. As we say back home in East Texas, I was as big as the side of the house. I had been overweight for about 10 years at that point, since the birth of my first child.

In less than a year, I basically lost the equivalent of a small person. I've been asked countless times what my secret is for losing that much weight. I think most people are slightly disappointed when I say that it was due to good old diet and exercise. Now, to be completely honest there was no real excuse for me being that large. I love food and I ate too much of everything. And I didn't exercise. Also, I'm not pointing fingers at you accusing you of the same thing. You know why you're overweight or unhealthy even if you're not willing to admit it to yourself, much less anyone else.

I came to the realization that even though I thought I'd tried to lose weight, I really hadn't put any real effort into it. I was lazy and made the decision to no longer let that be my excuse. I was under no delusions that I wasn't fat, but it took seeing a picture of myself on my 31st birthday to snap me back into reality.

What will it take to shock you into making a change for the better?

So, Why ARE you fat?

Have you ever asked yourself that question and given a completely honest answer? Let me address some of the reasons you may be overweight:

1. You eat the Standard American Diet (SAD)
2. You don't take supplements
3. You don't drink enough water
4. You don't exercise or you exercise sporadically
5. You have a chronic health issue that makes losing weight difficult
6. You've "tried everything and nothing worked"

The Standard American Diet is high in animal fats, saturated fats and in processed foods, but low in fiber, complex carbohydrates and plant based foods. Luckily, the SAD diet is easily reversed by making better food choices. The SAD diet is lacking in nutritionally dense foods.

Even if you eat a diet full of fruits, vegetables, whole grains, dairy, and lean, grass-fed beef, free range poultry, and wild caught fish, it's hard to get all the nutrients you need every day, thus the need for supplements. Taking a good multivitamin, essential fatty acids (EFAs), vitamin D, and antioxidants can fill in the gaps of even the best diet and really improve your health.

Are you well hydrated? I'm going to assume that you aren't. Most people aren't. Although the guidelines for how much water you need every day has changed in the past few years, I am a firm believer in a *minimum* of 64oz of pure water every day. If you're trying to lose weight, you should try to drink 96oz – every day. The Institute of Medicine recommends that women drink 91oz of water daily and men drink 125oz.

Every cell in your body needs water in order to function. Proper hydration ensures that every cell in your body functions optimally; it helps to regulate body temperature, helps your body eliminate wastes, lubricates and cushions your joints, and can increase your metabolism so that you burn more fat. Being even mildly dehydrated can cause headaches, fatigue and impaired concentration.

You can get about 20% of your daily fluid needs from the foods you eat but the rest should be from liquids. If you consume caffeinated beverages, adjust your water intake to at least the same amount of plain water throughout the day. Once you start drinking adequate amounts of water, your body will begin to crave it.

Don't Be a Victim of the "Diets Don't Work" Syndrome

I hate to be the bearer of bad news, but it's not the diet or exercise plans that didn't work; it's you that didn't. If you're a bit offended by that statement, ask yourself why. Granted, there are some very valid reasons why some people have a hard time becoming healthy and dropping excess weight but to jump on the "I can't lose weight" or "I've tried everything and nothing works" bandwagon is a self-fulfilling prophecy.

Very few people have health conditions which make it really hard or even impossible to lose weight. Certain medications can make losing weight difficult or cause fatigue so you don't have the energy to workout. If these are things you are dealing with, I know it can be daunting to get past these obstacles, especially when the scale doesn't budge. However, those things shouldn't be a reason not to get up and move on a regular basis. If this is you, don't focus on results; instead try to focus on effort and consistency. You know if you fall into this category; if you aren't sure, you probably don't.

My rule of thumb when talking with potential clients about starting a workout program is this: if you can walk up and down stairs (even with difficulty) or can get up from a seated position, then you have the basic muscular strength and minimum endurance to start exercising.

If I Can Do It, So Can You

Over the past 10 years when I tell people my weight loss story, their first response is often "That must have been *really* hard." In actuality, it wasn't. I made a decision to workout consistently and to eat better. And I didn't let anything deter me from doing those things. Sure, the workouts were hard and sometimes I had an internal struggle to choose the right foods, but taking the first step – making a firm decision and then pursuing it with fierce determination – made all the difference in my efforts actually working as opposed to the other times when I only 'tried'.

If you are open to a self induced reality check please ask yourself the following questions:

1. Have I given any fitness or weight management plan at least 30 days of consistent effort?
2. Did I follow the plan as closely as I could?
3. Do I think I'm worth the effort it takes in order to significantly improve my health?

If you've started a new regimen and get frustrated after a week or two because you didn't lost 10 lbs, or you can't quite run a mile (for example), don't give up easily. You didn't become deconditioned or unhealthy overnight so don't expect significant change to occur in less than 90 days. There are many sensible plans out there that will produce results if you follow them as closely as you can - within reason - and are honest with yourself about the amount of effort you're actually putting into changing your not so healthy habits.

The third question might seem somewhat odd, but a vast majority of people I've worked with over the years have low self-esteem and diminished self worth. I hope that if you fall into this category, you will find ways to be your own best cheerleader and, in turn, realize that your quality of life can be improved by taking good care of your health.

By taking care of you, then you'll have more to give to those you love and care about. You'll also have the energy to do and enjoy the things that are important to you. This was a major motivating factor in my physical transformation.

Getting Started

As a personal trainer I find myself repeating many of the same things to each client. I often tell my clients "Don't make it any harder than it needs to be." In fact, I wrote that in a previous paragraph! Some things are worth repeating. Starting on the path to better health is only as difficult as you make it. But you DO need to get started. So, first things first: take out your calendar and pick a date to get started, even if it's 30 days from now. Make the appointment with yourself now so that it's on your mental radar. Taking a few weeks to prepare isn't necessarily a bad thing. In my experience, those who make a game plan before starting a program are far more successful than those who haphazardly stumble into the process.

As you look at your calendar, assess what days and times are realistic for you to consistently workout. Ideally, you should skip a day between workouts in the beginning in order to allow full recovery. I don't recommend jumping into a 5 day a week program if you haven't been working out regularly for at least a month prior to starting a new plan. Once you know when you can fit exercise into your schedule, put those appointments with yourself on your calendar for the first month so when work, family and social obligations crop up, you'll already have your "me" time blocked out.

You should consider whether or not you are going to join a gym, hire a trainer (which I highly recommend for the novice exerciser), work out at home, start walking or running, or even try one of the popular DVD workout programs that are advertised everywhere these days.

Also, buy new shoes if your athletic shoes are more than a year old. Your knees will thank you. Few things motivate me to work out more than a spiffy new pair of shoes. I don't think you need fancy workout clothes but adding a few new pieces to your workout wardrobe can be motivating as well.

If you'll be working out at home, buy some basic equipment for your "home gym" such as 3, 5, and 8 lb dumbbells, a mat, and two or three resistance bands. I also recommend a fitness ball but they can take up a lot of room and if you have a small space you might want to skip getting one. You will also need to pick a weekend to clean out your fridge, cupboards and pantry of foods that you know are unhealthy or that you would possibly binge on. Throw it all into a garbage bag and then take the bag out of your house. Plan to do this the weekend before you start a weight management plan.

I don't recommend starting a new fitness plan and a new diet at the same time. For most people, doing that is too overwhelming. Start by exercising consistently for 30 days since that will be the thing most likely to fall by the wayside if your life suddenly becomes very busy. After 30 days, you should be ready to give your diet an overhaul.

Taking time to prepare will enhance your success!

Fitness 101 – The Basics

One of the most common questions that I am asked is how to start a fitness program. While the answer to that question can be long and drawn out, I'm a fan of keeping things simple and straightforward.

Pick up any magazine or even pull up your internet homepage and you will likely find the latest "miracle" weight loss pill or workout that guarantees results in no time at all and with minimal (if any) effort on your part. I spend a lot of time rolling my eyes at these claims.

Fitness magazines are the absolute worst with their advertisements for fat burners, diuretics, pre-workout enhancers and post-workout recovery concoctions, etc. Once you get past all of that, you still have articles about how to get fit in 4 weeks, lose your belly flab in 10 days, and the "Best Workout Ever." There is so much contradictory information out there and it's easy to be confused. I'm going to break it down for you in the simplest terms possible.

For a beginner or deconditioned person, start with 30 minutes of exercise 3 days per week for 30 days. An intermediate exerciser (one who works out semi-regularly) can do 30 minutes to 1 hour 3 days per week, or 30 minutes 5 days per week.

The key is to not do too much too soon. It's easy to become overwhelmed and/or even injure yourself by not easing into an exercise program. Stopping and starting a workout plan doesn't give you any kind of results at all.

By ramping up to incorporate exercise as a regular part of your schedule, you will eventually get the results that you're looking for. This is something I cannot stress enough.

A Well-Rounded Workout Plan

Once you've decided on when, where and what type of workouts you will do, time to evaluate your plan to make sure you're covering all the basics of a well-rounded fitness plan. Every workout does not have to include all the components listed below, but in a weekly plan you should cover all of those basics.

The 5 components of a complete fitness plan include:

- Warmup (5-10 minutes of cardio such as walking or jogging, elliptical, bike, etc)
- Cardiovascular training
- Total body strength training
- Cool down
- Stretching

For the beginning exerciser on a three day per week plan it could look something like this:

Sample Basic Fitness Plan

Monday	Wednesday	Friday
Warm up	Warm up	Warm up
Cardio (20 minutes)	Cardio (20-30 minutes)	Cardio (20 minutes)
Strength Training (10 minutes)		Strength Training (10 minutes)
Cool Down	Cool Down	Cool Down
Stretching	Stretching	Stretching

As you can see, the above basic plan includes 3 days of cardio and two days of total body strength training. Anyone can find time to incorporate this into their schedule.

A 5 day split workout schedule in which you do cardio three days a week and strength training on two days would look like this:

<u>**Sample Workout Plan – Beginner to Intermediate**</u>

Monday/Wednesday/Friday

Warm up (5 minutes)

Cardio (20-30 minutes)

Cool Down (5 minutes)

Stretching (3-5 minutes minimum)

Tuesday/Thursday

Warm Up (5 minutes)

Strength Training (20 minutes)

Cool Down (5 minutes)

Stretching (3-5 minutes minimum)

The American Heart Association recommends 30 minutes to 1 hour of physical activity at least 5 days a week. Anyone can find at least 30 minutes to exercise at least three times a week. Billionaire Richard Branson, founder of the Virgin brand of businesses, and who is arguably busier than you or I, attributes his productivity to the fact that he makes it a priority to exercise. So what excuse do you have that you're too busy to work out?

Diet 101 – You Have to Eat to Lose

You must eat to lose weight. I know this is not what you think of when you think of the word "diet". Most people think of a severely limited number of calories and foods. As you know, a diet refers to the foods that you eat, whatever they might be. The perfect weight loss diet is the one you can stick to, whether you cut fat, carbohydrates, or some combination of the two. We're all smart enough to have a basic idea of what a healthy diet consists of so I won't go into that just yet.

Your body is a machine and can't function properly without the right fuel or being fueled often enough. How do you know for sure that you're getting adequate (or too many) calories? You don't know unless you keep a food diary or some kind of food/calorie tracker.

This can be a real eye opener. If you aren't eating enough, you'll see that. If you are overeating, that will be clear as well. Plus, if you're honest with yourself you won't want to write down that you ate half a pack of Oreos or a whole large bag of chips and it should help you make better choices.

Research has shown time and again that keeping track of what and how much you eat will not only help you lose more weight but also maintain your weight loss. Keeping a food diary can be as simple as recording what you eat in a Word document or even a tiny notebook that you can carry with you. There are also many smartphone apps which allow you to keep track of your food intake.

Weight Loss Rule #1: Eat Foods You Like

If you have ever bought a diet book or went to a weight loss center or decided to try the latest surefire fad diet, the common theme is too few calories, little variety, or pre-packaged "plastic" food. The diet and weight loss industry is a multi-billion dollar per year industry. People tend to believe anything they read on a label or just want a quick fix, which doesn't work.

Would you be able to stick to a plan that requires you to eat foods that you don't like? I have clients that will not eat pork or broccoli or hate vegetables. Any plan can be modified within reason to better suit your palate. Simply trade a serving of protein for a different protein, and so forth.

Weight Loss Rule #2: Eat Several Small Meals a Day

Any food plan worth following will typically recommend eating 5 to 6 times a day. You should strive to eat often enough that you never feel hungry. Try spacing your meals every 3-4 hours so that you never get to the point where you feel ravenous.

Eating often keeps the fat furnace burning all day and should keep you from cheating or binging from deprivation or hunger. When you eat, your metabolism revs up to digest your food (digestion is a high calorie-burning activity). Waiting too long between meals causes your metabolism to tank. Then you eat again and it goes up. It's a metabolic roller coaster, not unlike a yo-yo diet.

A daily eating plan would include a normal breakfast, lunch and dinner with a snack mid-morning and mid-afternoon; and possibly an after dinner snack depending on whether or not you tend to feel hungry a few hours after your last meal.

Do you notice a pattern? Never let yourself get so hungry that you would eat anything and everything you can get your hands on.

Weight Loss Rule #3: Eating Too Few Calories Slows Your Metabolism

Restricting too many calories for more than several days causes your body to go into "starvation mode". This is why dieters hit the dreaded plateau over the course of an excessively restrictive diet. Your body is a truly intelligent machine. When you stop eating adequate calories for your body to function optimally, your metabolism slows down and your ability to lose weight becomes almost impossible. Over time you would need to eat less and less in order to lose, or not gain, weight. That's not healthy or maintainable for anyone.

The number of calories you should eat per day depends on your height, body type, age, and activity level. A simple guideline is no less than 1200 calories a day for women (unless you're short – 5' 2" or under, you can get away with 1000 calories per day) and 1800 calories per day for men; the more active you are, the more calories you need.

Diet plans that require you to eat so little that you're constantly starving give you no incentive to stay on them since the tendency to cheat is so high. I don't know anyone who enjoys starving. I don't, and I would never succeed on any plan where I couldn't eat enough to not be hungry all the time. Nor will you.

Eat Clean – Lose Fat

How many fad diets have you tried in the past? The majority of fad diets are typically nutritionally unbalanced and focuses on extreme food and calorie restriction or excessive consumption of just a few foods. The Cabbage Soup Diet, Lemonade Diet, HCG diet, Grapefruit diet, and Hollywood Diet (you drink a "miracle juice" that help you magically drop pounds) are just a few examples.

I don't recommend prepackaged food diets such as Nutrisystem or Jenny Craig. In order to learn how to make better food choices you must prepare your own meals instead of relying on pre-portioned prepared foods.

The best diet is not a "diet" at all but consistently (there's that word again!) making good choices. Make the healthiest choices you can 80% of the time. I'm giving you permission to cheat occasionally. No food is off limits but don't think you can eat junk food every day and hope to be healthy and fit. Once or twice a week won't derail any diet as long as you pay close attention to portion sizes of your favorite non-diet foods.

Clean eating is a plan based on eating whole foods, or foods that are closest to their natural state. This means eating plenty of fresh vegetables and fruits, grass fed meats when possible, hormone free dairy, and significantly reducing your intake of saturated fat and eliminating as much processed sugar as possible. Processed, prepackaged foods as well as fast foods should be avoided as much as possible.

On the average day, strive to make the following foods and serving amounts the basis of your diet:

Food	Servings Per Day
Protein	5 – 6 three to four ounce portions
Breads/Grains/Cereals/Starches	3 -4 whole grains
Vegetables	5 servings + unlimited greens
Fruits	2 – 3 medium
Dairy	3-4 four to eight ounce servings
Fats	5 -6 servings
Water	64 – 96oz

I'm not a calorie counter and I'm not into weighing my food. Instead, I go by number of portions of foods per day to keep track of what I'm eating. Websites and apps that count your calories are nice but a trend that I've noticed with clients over and over again is that people tend to become laser focused on the number of calories they consume.

While this information is helpful it's not a complete picture of overall macronutrient intake. An apple and a handful of crackers can have the same number of calories but nutritionally, the apple is a far better choice. So, beware that all calories are NOT created equal. Again, whole foods as opposed to packaged and processed foods have the vitamins, minerals, fiber, phytochemicals, and antioxidants that your body needs. A pack of Twizzlers, for example, certainly doesn't, even if they happen to be "fat free" and made with "natural" ingredients.

Real food equals real nutrition, which is what your body is really craving. As you make eating whole, clean foods the basis of your diet you will notice that you don't crave junk food. There are also other benefits of eating well which can't be measured on the scale, such as increased energy and endurance, better moods, etc.

The Bottom Line – Real Change IS Attainable

The amazing Jack Lalanne once said, "How do you build up your bank account? By putting something in it every day. Your health account is no different. What I do today, I am wearing tomorrow. If I put inferior foods in my body today, I'm going to be inferior tomorrow, it's that simple."

No matter what fitness or weight management plan you choose to follow, just get started. There is no 'one size fits all' diet or fitness regimen. Don't think about it too much- just get up and move several days a week and make healthy food choices 80% of the time.

There are literally hundreds of plans out there to try but the bottom line is that none of them will work unless you do. There is no substitute for putting in the time and effort. If there was, someone would have discovered it by now.

As stated earlier, the future is now. Be your own best doctor and take care of your health. No one else can do it for you. There is no such thing as perfection, so don't waste your precious time and energy beating yourself up because you're not perfect.

Commit to consistently make better choices and you will not only improve your health and quality of life, but also lower your risk for many diseases by making your health a priority.

It won't happen overnight, but it will happen with consistent effort. And believe me, I know you're worth it!

SABRINA PETERSON

Sabrina is a National Academy of Sports Medicine Certified Personal Trainer and Corrective Exercise specialist. In 2001 she weighed 291 lbs and wore size 26 clothes. Since losing 120lbs she has helped countless others become healthier, happier and "afters" as well. She has owned and operated an in-home personal training business since 2006 and works with clients of all ages and fitness levels. Her specialization is working with clients who are seriously overweight, severely deconditioned, injury prone, and those training for athletic competition. She has worked with clients as young as 19 and as old as 89. The best thing about her job is that she gets to help people every day! She is also a proud mom of three amazing children who help keep her young.

www.sabrinapeterson.com